THAT'S ENTERTAINMENT

A HUNDRED YEARS OF DUNFERMLINE OPERA HOUSE

LILLIAN KING

RESEARCH BY BRIAN NOBILE

ISBN NO: 0 9539839 3 5

Acknowledgements

For Belle, as always

I would like to express my gratitude to everyone who contributed in any way to this book.
Special thanks go to

The Carnegie Dunfermline Trust for funding
Brian Nobile, whose idea it was and who provided the original research
Gordon Ellis, Bill Gourlay
Denise Coffey, Freda Drysdale
Brenda Kucharewski
Iain Mackintosh, Theatre Consultants, Sir James Dunbar-Nasmith,
Ian Terris, Frank and Margaret Tait,
Susan Melum, Asolo Theatre
Linda Rosenbluth, Sarasota Sister Cities Association
Local History Staff at the Carnegie Library, Dunfermline

Research by Brian Noble
Additional research by Lillian King

© Lillian King July 2003

Cover design by Belle Hammond
Printed by Envoy Printers, Rosyth
Typesetting, layout and design by Windfall Books
Published by Windfall Books

Opera House audiences

JOHNNY BEATTIE

When the question of a foreword for this book came up, there was only one name to be considered. Johnny Beattie is one of the most popular and enduring names in show business, and has celebrated a remarkable fifty years in front of the footlights.

His career encompasses everything from Music Hall, pantomime and variety theatre to television quizzes, Hogmanay Specials and now soap opera – BBC's River City. His show 'From Broadway to Cowdenbeath' *attracted rave reviews at the 2002 Edinburgh International Festival. The title refers to an episode in 1959 when he returned to Scotland after performing at the Waldorf Astoria in New York, and was told his next gig was at the Miners Institute in Cowdenbeath.*

Johnny is still very much in demand as a performer, and is still making people laugh after half a century, so we are delighted and honoured that he has taken time out from his very busy schedule to write this foreword.

FOREWORD

My first appearance in the Opera House was in 1953. As a young performer just starting in the business it was a magical experience. The theatre had a wonderful atmosphere, thanks mainly to the unique baroque style decor in the auditorium. I was hooked immediately. Topping the bill on that occasion were Tommy Hope and Jimmy Lang. Every night I had the pleasure of watching these two masters of comedy, looking, listening and learning.

The following year, I appeared with Billy Stutt, a very funny Irish comedian, and Stan Mars, an up and coming Scots comic, who became a lifelong friend. Happy memories, indeed!

I remember, too, with great fondness, the kindness shown to me as a young performer by the theatre's musical director, Arthur Lax. The theatre manager at that time was Mr Robert Walker, a man very much in touch with all that went on in the local community. He gave the classic excuse for a drop in the business one week.

'It was,' he said, 'the end of the Co-operative quarter.'

This book affords readers a fascinating glimpse into the illustrious history of the Opera House. The roll call of performers and musicians, and the shows in which they appeared, is meticulously detailed.

There are some gems of information in these pages. The great illusionist and hypnotist Doctor Walford Bodie MD, started out in life as Sam Murphy. 'What's in a name?' they say. He claimed in court that the letters MD after his name stood for Merry Devil.

On one occasion, a local amateur drama group presented a play with the mind boggling title *Six Pass While the Lentils Boil*. Could this have been the forerunner of kitchen sink drama?

These stories and many others have been painstaking documented by the author. Contributions from artists and public alike about memorable shows and favourite performers give readers a wonderful insight into what made the Opera House a very special place of entertainment.

It is of some consolation that the beautiful interior of the grand old theatre lives on in Sarasota, Florida. Appropriately enough, Sarasota is Dunfermline's twin city in America, with strong Scottish connections - a fascinating story in itself.

In writing and researching this book, obviously a labour of love, Lillian King has made a valuable contribution to the history of the Scottish theatre.

Johnny Beattie!

CONTENTS

INTRODUCTION

In July, 2000, an exhibition was held in Abbot House, Dunfermline. *They Played Dunfermline* was a celebration of one hundred years of entertainment in the town. It marked two anniversaries - one hundred years since the go-ahead was given to build the town's most famous theatre in Reform Street, Dunfermline, and forty five years since the last ever performance there.

Brian Nobile who had spent years amassing material relating to The Dunfermline Opera House and other local entertainment venues, unveiled his huge collection of memorabilia, which included posters, handbills, photographs and press cuttings.

On show was material donated by local people in response to newspaper coverage, and letters from many of the big names in the entertainment world who had performed in The Opera House and other venues in Dunfermline.

A few months earlier, in April that year, The Dunfermline Press had carried a report that the town of Sarasota in Florida was planning to seek 'sister city' links with Dunfermline. An unlikely pairing, you might think, but the two towns already had very strong links.

Sarasota was founded by Scots. Sir John Hamilton Gillespie, an Edinburgh Writer to the Signet, a member of The Royal Company of Archers and a Director of the Edinburgh Academy, had formed the Florida Mortgage and Investment company, which owned fifty thousand acres around Sarasota Bay. In 1885 emigrants from Scotland, lured with promises of good houses, fertile land and citrus groves, left Glasgow for a new life. They found a settlement with no streets or houses and had to sleep in makeshift tents. Being Scots, however, they didn't give up easily. Though some returned to Scotland and others moved north to Tampa and New York, many stayed.

Gillespie's son was sent out to oversee the colony and he later built a hotel and what is thought to be one of America's first golf courses. By 1910 Sarasota had developed into a popular holiday destination and remains so to this day. The city celebrates Tartan Day, has its own Caledonian Society and its High School Kiltie Band is well known throughout America.

Sarasota has had a long involvement with the entertainment industry. One of its most famous sons is John Ringling, one of seven brothers who owned eleven circuses. The Ringling Brothers Circus merged with Barnum and Bailey and John became its sole director in 1930. He later established a Museum of American Circus and Arts Museum in Sarasota.

The city's centenary celebrations were due to take place in 2002 and it was suggested that this was an appropriate time to formalise the proposed link with Dunfermline. Apart from the wider Scottish connection, Sarasota already had a very positive link with the Fife town.

In 1987, the interior of Dunfermline Opera House, which had been built in Reform Street in 1903 and dismantled in 1981, was transported to Florida to become part of The Asolo Centre for Performing Arts complex.

What made the Opera House so special was that only a few baroque style Scottish theatres, built around the turn of the century, survive.

Among those still in use are the Perth Theatre, designed by Roy Jackson, who later used aspects of its design in the Reform Street building; the King's Theatre in Glasgow, built in 1904 and its namesake in Edinburgh , built the following year.

One very unusual feature of the Opera House was its *soffit* or decorated elliptical arch above the orchestra pit.

Rare in Britain, this is sometimes seen in American theatres built around the same time by architect Thomas Lamb. He had been born in Scotland but emigrated to America as a child.

In January 1990, ninety years after plans for the Opera House were first approved, Dunfermline Provost, James Cameron, joined Burt Reynolds and other prominent Sarasota citizens attending the grand opening ceremony of the new Asolo Main Stage, an almost perfect replica of the interior of Dunfermline's famous theatre.

The history of a hundred years of theatre has been captured in Brian Nobile's collection and in material held by The Carnegie Library Dunfermline, and The Dunfermline Press who have kindly granted permission for its use.

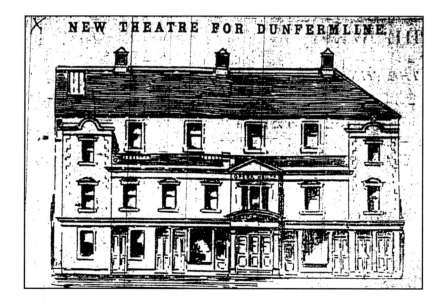

The original plans for the Opera House submitted in 1900

CHAPTER ONE

A BOON FOR THE DISTRICT

On Saturday August 22, 1903, The Dunfermline Journal announced that the town's new theatre would open on September 10th. Like the good time in the old song, the report said, it had been a long time coming. Just how long it took from the initial idea is hard to say but permission to build the theatre to be known as The Opera House was given in August 1900 in spite of opposition by neighbouring proprietors in Reform Street.

Plans had been drawn up by Roy Jackson, an architect and theatrical manager from Perth and the construction work was carried out by Messrs George and John Anderson of Dunfermline. It was to be an imposing building of stone and brick, 'eighty three feet long, with centre gable and tower at either side and a moulded pediment over the main entrance.'

This was to have an ornamental verandah projecting on to the pavement. The theatre would seat one thousand two hundred and fifty people and all areas would have a perfect view of the stage. This was to be achieved by the circle and balcony tiers being built on the cantilever principle, thus doing away with the normal pillars.

The Journal was very enthusiastic. 'The theatre, which will be lighted by gas, when completed will be one of the prettiest and most comfortable in the provinces,' it said, 'and with a population of about fifty thousand in Dunfermline and in the vil

lages round about, there is no doubt that the theatre should be a great boon to the district.'

Dunfermline was already well catered for as far as entertainment was concerned. In January, St Margaret's Hall had been the venue for Professor E.K. Crocker's educated horses and 'a trip to the moon in thirty scenes'.

Edison's New Electric Animated pictures showed The Great Delhi Durbar, and 'leagues and leagues' of Canadian pictures.

Anyone tired of local entertainment could go to one of Edinburgh's theatres or pop into India Buildings and get married immediately by special licence.

Nevertheless, those planning the theatre were confident that they could compete, but it was not all plain sailing. In order to provide space for the new building, some old houses had to be demolished and the walls of others facing the street were grafted into the front of the new building. The cost rose from the original estimate of five thousand to six thousand pounds.

Safety was very much a priority. There were several exits and entrances all of which led to Reform Street and so arranged that in an emergency the house could be cleared in a matter of minutes.

Stairways were designed to prevent as far as possible anyone slipping over the steps. Capable of seating thirteen hundred patrons, the auditorium

New Opera House

Dunfermline

Proprietor .... G & G Anderson
General Manager .... Mr W. E. Potts

OPENING BY THE

Dunfermline Amateur Dramatic Club

And

Mr. Walter Bentley

Under the distinguished patronage of

Andrew Carnegie, Esq., of Skibo Castle, Hon. President.
Sir James Sivewright of Tulliallan Castle, Hon. Vice-President.
Provost Scobie, Hon. Vice-President.
Bailie Stewart, Hon, Vice-President
The Magistrates and Town Council Of Dunfermline and the local gentry

Friday And Saturday 11th & 12th September 1903

When the Two Clever Plays will be produced

A FRIEND IN NEED

And the Famous Scotch Drama

CRAMOND BRIG

Plan of Seats at Liddell's (formely Clark & Son's) High Street

The Formal Grand Professional Opening will take place on
Thursday, Friday and Saturday
17th, 18th, 19th September 1903
With The

J. W. Turner's
Grand English Company

Playbill for Opening Night

was divided into the dress circle with two private boxes, the upper circle, stalls, pit and gallery.

The Anderson brothers owned and built the theatre and the manager, Mr W.E. Potts, superintended the interior arrangements.

Potts had begun his career as a programme boy in The Lyceum Theatre in Sunderland. Later he joined the company of Charles Dillon, one of the finest actors of the time. Before coming to Dunfermline he had been business manager of the famous Milton-Rays Companies and had also leased a theatre in Dumfries.

The private boxes were tiered, the first arrangement of its kind in this country, and provided a clear view of the stage for nine or ten people instead of the usual four. Crimson was the predominating colour of the upholstery for their luxurious fittings. The dress circle, with tip up seats supplied by Deans, theatrical furnishers of Birmingham, was also decked in crimson cloth and velvet.

The stalls also had tip up seats, and for people who could not afford to pay more than the humble sixpence, there were comfortable seats in the gallery. This had a heavy iron railing along the front to prevent 'too adventurous spirits from being the cause of an accident.'

Robert Wood, a painter and authority on theatre decoration was responsible for the scheme of decoration and adorned the fronts of the dress circle and gallery with bands of ornamental scroll work in duresco, relieved with gold. He was also responsible for the ceiling design.

The stage, with a proscenium arch of twenty four by twenty six feet, was capable of taking in the scenery of any touring company and all the latest scene shifting appliances were installed.

Claud Broadbridge painted the backdrop and the scenery, which would be lighted from above by three specially designed batten lights as well as by footlights. The main lighting came from a huge 'gasalier' suspended from the centre of the ceiling, and fitted with one of the latest forms of incandescent light. Heating was by means of hot water pipes, and a ventilator was installed to keep the air sweet.

The writer in The Dunfermline Journal looked back on the days when the theatre was regarded as an enemy of the church, and was happy that opinions had now changed. He went further, claiming that the actor, 'by his living impersonations, may do as much to elevate the lives of the masses as the minister.'

No-one, he says, now denies the educative influence of pure drama. Dr Carnegie, who he believed 'was more endowed with Christian graces than the most of us' had expressed his support for the theatre as long as only the purest plays were allowed to find expression within her temple.

Whether Carnegie was speaking about theatre in Dunfermline or simply theatre in general is unclear, but over the years a legend has sprung up that the great philanthropist was involved in the building of The Opera House. In fact the only connection is coincidental. The Dunfermline Carnegie Trust was formed in August 1903 and The Opera House opened the following month.

One reason for the erroneous belief may be that Carnegie was a patron of Dunfermline Amateur Dramatic Society. Already a very thriving company, it was chosen for the theatre's opening performance on September 11, 1903.

According to the next day's newspapers, 'their production was given under the distinguished patronage of Mr Andrew Carnegie, Honorary President, Sir James Sivewright, Tulliallan Castle, Provost Scobie and Bailie Stewart, Vice Presidents; and Magistrates and Town Council of Dunfermline.'

Two plays, *A Friend in Need* and *Cramond Brig* were presented and the Dunfermline Journal was not altogether complimentary about the performance.

In an article entitled *Hansel Night*, it said, 'Opinions may differ as to whether in their own interests, the proprietors of the new Opera House in Dunfermline ought to have secured a professional or an amateur company to open the tidy little theatre in Reform Street. Undoubtedly, a number of members of the combination possess histrionic abilities and, if further trained might do credit to any stage; but to speak the truth, and it is done in kindness, some people ought not to allow themselves to be stage stricken.'

The local company, it went on, 'essayed to shed sweetness and light but whether they did so remained a moot point. Talent there was, certainly, but the efforts of some might be better not displayed before the footlights. Nervousness or stage fright might have contributed and a better performance was expected the following night. Even the theatre cat did not escape the drama critic - it was said to be useful, if not obedient.

One of the boxes was occupied by Sir James Sivewright, who made a short but appropriate speech in the interval, and the other by Mrs Stenhouse of Linburn and a party of friends.

It is unlikely that Carnegie ever attended one of the Dramatic Society's performances but his patronage continued and later Opera House adverts carried a quote from him:

'The theatre has come to stay and it devolves upon us to avail itself of its tremendous power for good. The best way for good people to aid and improve the theatre is to patronise it.'

On September 19th, the paper reported the professional opening of the Opera House with a marked difference in tone to the previous week's item. The formal gala opening took place on the seventeenth, with J.W. Turner's Grand English Opera Company and a performance of *The Bohemian Girl*. This was followed the next two nights by *Faust* and *Maritana*.

The opera had a magnificent reception with every part of the trig little theatre being filled, and the reporter's only complaint was that the audience tended to overdo their appreciation. However, the writer went on to single out the chorus and almost every character for praise. According to him, nothing superior to the beautiful dresses and the 'Tyrolese garbs' were ever witnessed in the city, and the whole performance was really a credit to the company.

Visiting companies often did their own publicity and the great American Indian play *On The Frontier* had its own Indian and cowboy band that paraded through the town every day. The number of touring companies that advertised their show as having come direct from one of the many theatres in London speaks volumes for the business acumen of the manager and the quality of the accommodation.

There were no problems in some shows about patrons arriving late. They could get in for half price at nine o'clock, though the show began at seven forty five. The variety of shows on offer was phenomenal, from F.R. Fenson's Shakespearian Company to Marston and Buckstone's light comedies, 'replete with the most charming musical novelties and dances of the day.' Mr William Greet's company introduced the cakewalk in *The Lady Slavey*.

Historical scenes were popular. 'Don't miss the Battle of Trafalgar and the death of Nelson,' said the playbills for *The Mariners of England* and *The Days of Nelson*. From The *Gay Parisienne* to *Life in Louisiana* and plays about Boer farmers, horizons continued to be widened.

Performers were referred to formally and were always 'celebrated' or 'acclaimed.' In *The Royal Divorce, A Story of Waterloo*, Miss Elizabeth Watson as the Empress Josephine was supported by Mr George W. Cockburn as Napoleon, and each lady in the audience was presented with 'a magnificent souvenir containing life-like portraits of Napoleon and Josephine.'

In February 1904, Fred Karno paid his first visit to the Opera House with his famous company of comedians. They had earlier performed as a tumbling act in the St Margaret's Halls.

Karno began his career as a circus trapeze act, became a ringmaster and clown, and toured Europe before being asked to deputise for an acrobatic act called *The Three Carnos* in London. He changed his name to Karno and by 1897 was an established music hall act.

By the turn of the century he had five companies on the road. Billed as *Fred Karno's Speechless Comedians* they were a knockabout mime act. *His Majesty's Guests,* which he brought to Dunfermline in 1904 was his first spoken production.

It was 'a series of situations arranged and invented by Karno, with sparkling music, beautiful dresses, pretty girls, refined comedy and charming dances.' His most famous sketch *Mumming Birds* which also came to The Opera House was booked for an eight week season in New York.

It ran, on and off, for over nine years .Karno built his own 'Karsino' but went bankrupt in 1936 and went back to variety, still using the *Mumming Birds* sketch.

Karno was a household name. During the first World War, 'Fred Karno's Army,' sung to the tune of the Church's One Foundation, became a popular marching tune:

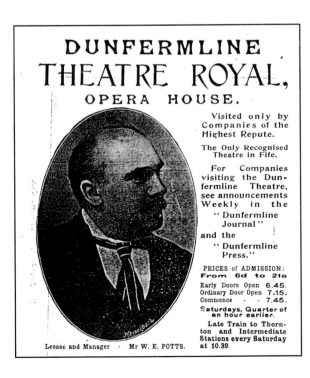

DUNFERMLINE THEATRE ROYAL, OPERA HOUSE.

Visited only by Companies of the Highest Repute.

The Only Recognised Theatre in Fife.

For Companies visiting the Dunfermline Theatre, see announcements Weekly in the " Dunfermline Journal " and the " Dunfermline Press."

PRICES of ADMISSION: From 6d to 21s.
Early Doors Open 6.45.
Ordinary Door Open 7.15.
Commence - - 7.45.
Saturdays, Quarter of an hour earlier.
Late Train to Thornton and Intermediate Stations every Saturday at 10.39.

Lessee and Manager · Mr W. E. POTTS.

We are Fred Karno's army,
A jolly lot are we
Fred Karno is our captain
Charles Chaplin our OC
And when we get to Berlin
The Kaiser he will say
Hoch. Hoch. Mein Gott.
What a jolly fine lot
Are the boys of Company A.

One of his most successful shows was *The Love Match,* with Jean Alliston, wife of comedian Tommy Handley, and supported by twenty foxhounds, rabbits, ferrets, four thoroughbred greys and a talking horse. In 1935 he formed his own film company but only made one film with Rob Wilton which was not a success.

Among the comedians Fred employed were Max Miller, Charlie Chaplin, Sandy Powell, Flanagan and Allen, and Stan Laurel. After retiring from the stage, Fred ran a wine shop till his death in 1941.

More serious fare than Fred's knockabout style was normal for Dunfermline. For three days in March 1904, Miss Ella Forrest and her Company presented *The Curate*, which probably matched the criteria suggested by Andrew Carnegie. Today it seems to epitomise the melodramatic taste of the age. The villain, hero, and beautiful damsel in distress are all here along with deathbed scenes, bravery in battle, and an obligatory bittersweet ending. The programme notes are fascinating.

Act One - The Village Homestead - The blind father and his daughter

Act Two - The Mesmerist at Work - She has killed her own father but he loves her still - Minister, I am dying. Take my hand and swear by all you hold sacred to find my child and save her from herself.

Act Three - Outside the Church - The abandoned one. The snake and the curate meet face to face. Never friendless when I am by her side, never homeless whilst the church can shelter her.

Act Four - By the Camp Fire in the Crimean Trenches. The curate saves the snake's life.

During this scene a number of specialities will be introduced. Up to date songs and dances. Miss Ella Forrest, the well known elocutionist will recite Clement Scottt's 'Midnight Charge'

Act Five - A Russian dagger and a British Fist - death of Dick the Trumpeter, the bravest little heart in the regiment. The snake finds his match and the curate finds a sweetheart.

And not a dry eye in the house.

As a complete contrast, for the next three days, the company performed Uncle Tom's Cabin. At the same time, over in St Margaret's Hall, two hundred children were performing J.G. Grieve's *Kinderspiel, Don Quixote*

Neither St Margaret's nor The Opera House, however, could compete with what must have been the most spectacular entertainment ever to visit Fife. In August 1904, Buffalo Bill's Wild West Show came to town before going on to visit Kirkcaldy and Dundee.

Three special trains brought five hundred horses and eight hundred people. These included one hundred North American Indians, an Imperial Japanese troupe, a congress of the rough riders of the world, gauchos, vaqueros, Bedouin Arabs, Cuban patriots and Russian Cossacks.

Among the treats on offer were the Battle of The Little Big Horn, Custer's Last Stand, and one intrepid cowboy cyclist who could jump over an abyss fifty six feet wide.

According to the newspaper report, many people had stayed up all night to get a ticket for the show which had so impressed Queen Victoria that she had commanded Buffalo Bill to appear at Windsor.

In Dunfermline, however, some parts of the show had a mixed reception. This presumably was caused by an awareness of the war that was raging in the Far East between Russia and Japan over attempts to colonise Korea and Manchuria.

The Japanese were cheered when they appeared but silence greeted the Cossacks. By the end of their act, however, they were cheered as loudly as any other performer.

At the end of the spectacular entertainment a concert was given by a company of artistes. The side shows afterwards had 'the usual concomitant of all great gatherings, a number of professional mendicants who, minus an upper or lower limb, sought to excite pity and extort charity.'

The same week, another 'first' for the town, though on a much smaller scale, was a two day visit by Harry Lauder to St Margaret's Hall.

Described as Scotland's representative entertainer, he was supported by a specially selected company of high class artistes. Lauder visited both Kelty and Cowdenbeath and, presumably, performed there as well as appearing in Dunfermline.

Lauder was born in Portobello in 1840 and entered Band of Hope talent contests and charity shows while still at school. Later he became a flax mill worker, and worked as a miner for ten years before deciding to try his luck on the stage.

He toured with concert parties before teaming up with Mackenzie Murdoch to form the 'Lauder-Murdoch Concert Party.'

His first performances in England were as an Irish singer and he only began singing Scottish songs when he ran out of Irish material. London usually meant sudden death for Scots comedians, but if Dan Leno could appear at the Glasgow Empire, singing English songs for a hundred pounds a week, Lauder thought he might be able to get ten pounds a week in London singing Scots songs.

His first London appearance was in 1900. He was an overnight success and within a few years he was touring America and being regarded as the most successful artiste the variety stage had ever known.

He was one of vaudeville's greatest attractions for over thirty years, and toured Australia, New Zealand and South Africa.

OPERA HOUSE

REFORM STREET

THREE NIGHTS!

MONDAY, TUESDAY & WEDNESDAY

Mr Fred Karno's Coy. Of Comedians

IN

HIS MAJESTY'S GUESTS

An exhilarating Extravaganza – Bristling with Novelties

Sparkling Music!   *Beautiful Dresses!*
    Pretty Girls!   *Refined Comedy*
    Charming Dances! Picturesque Scenery!
Witty Dialogues!   *Roars of Laughter!*

Chorus under the Orchestra Direction of Ernest Wolfe.

Business and Situations arranged and invented by Mr Fred Karno

Playbill for Saturday February 6th, 1904

Turned down for active service, he performed up to six front line concerts a day and was knighted in 1919 for his services to the theatre and especially for his work as a wartime entertainer

Though he retired in 1935, Lauder again entertained the troops during the second world war and was President of the Scottish Regional Committee of ENSA. He died in 1950.

Shortly after Lauder's visit, the theatre which had been closed for several weeks, re-opened with a new name, Theatre Royal and Opera House, and under the personal management of W. E. Potts, now the new owner.

Several alterations had been made to the interior of the building, especially the gallery which was now in two parts, the amphitheatre or front gallery and the back gallery. This alteration provided 'most comfortable seating and a clear view of the stage.'

Once again the grand opening was by J.W. Turner's Grand Opera company, this time with performances of *The Puritan's Daughter*, *Il Trovatore* and *Maritana*.

Performers came from far afield. *The Kilties*, Canada's greatest concert band, appeared in April 1905, and earlier in the year patrons had been offered a performance of 'a previously unpublished episode in the career of Sherlock Holmes, direct from The Lyceum Theatre, London.'

In October, one of the most important and costly engagements of the season introduced Mrs Bandmann-Palmer and her company, who performed *School for Scandal, Mary Queen of Scots* and *Sapho*. There was also a presentation of Hamlet with the only lady Hamlet on the British stage.

Theatrical touring companies were the mainstay

of the theatre and these were interspersed with light opera, benefit and club nights.

Performances were given by the local Amateur Dramatic Society for charities such as The Female Beneficent Society, or the cottage hospital. There were also a number of benefit performances for Mr Potts. One in April 1906, billed as the greatest event of the year, included a production of *Rob Roy*, which was supported by the town band.

Harry Lauder

Another, the following year, featured three plays, *A Breach of Promise* with the last public appearance of 'the Laughing Nigger'; *Delicate Ground* with Miss Madge Locke, 'the favourite Chanteuse and Terpsichorean Expert,' and a new Scottish comic romance *My Heart's in the Highlands*.

Some plays seemed to be more popular than others, with the performers at least. *East Lynne* appeared regularly as did *The Shaughraun* and *Jeanie Deans*. Others went in for spectacular effects. *The Still Alarm* purported to be a 'great American drama' and featured beautifully trained horses, a steam fire engine and a New York Central fire station.

Many plays contained vaudeville scenes either integral to the plot, or shown during intervals and scene changes.

In November, a great treat was promised. The British Empire Talking Pictures and Variety Show offered a programme to suit all classes with sport, travel, comic and dramatic pictures.

Films were used as part of variety bills from the beginning of the century but talking pictures? Everyone knows the first talkie *The Jazz Singer* appeared in 1926. Or were they around twenty years earlier?

In December 1906, Mahomed, the only Egyptian actor author, and his full vaudeville company, were appearing for two nights. Alongside advertisements for lectures and recitals was one for a women's suffrage meeting. It was to be the first of many.

The Press's front pages give odd and quirky insights into daily life. The Carnegie Dunfermline Trust had been formed in 1903, just one month before the Opera House opened .

If the theatre was concerned only with entertainment, there was practically no area of life that the Trust was not involved in – concerts by local and national orchestras and opera companies, amateur dramatics, gardening, women's institutes, swimming, athletics, music and elocution classes, exhibitions and lectures on an amazing variety of subjects.

In January 1908, beside an Opera House advert for *A Girl Redeemed From Sin* - some companies had a fondness for moralistic tales - and one for a ploughing match at Crossgates, is another for *What a City Sanitary Inspector Does*, in St Margaret's Hall.

In February Celtic played Raith Rovers at Starks Park and in April while the Christy Minstrels were appearing at St Margaret's Hall a native choir from Jamaica, described as twelve coloured ladies and gentlemen all educated to a high order, performed in The Opera House.

The Women's Freedom League held meetings in the run up to the election and the Scottish Prohibition Party presented Mrs Carry A. Nation, America's saloon smasher. She brought her hatchet with her and described 'How I smashed, why I smashed, how you may smash.' If that didn't appeal, you could attend a Theosophy lecture on *After Death Conditions*.

In the same year, old age pensions were introduced. Fraser's grocer shop celebrated this by offering every fiftieth customer their groceries free. Horn gramophones and disc machines were in the shops with Harry Lauder's new recordings.

The latest craze at the ice rink was waltzing. The Rink at Canmore Street held fancy dress carnivals among its other attractions. At holiday time, pleasure steamers made trips daily, weather permitting, from Charlestown to Aberdour and Leith.

In 1910, Mr Potts was granted a licence to show films, extensive alterations were carried out in the theatre, and he negotiated with The Electric Theatre Company for their latest and most up to date productions. Heads of families were advised to 'watch this paper each week.'

The first pictures were shown in April, and films and variety programmes were to continue to run alongside each other. Special cheap theatre trains were organised on Saturday evenings from Lochgelly, Crossgates and Halbeath.

In August, adverts appeared for what was described as 'Forbes Robertson's great play *The Passing of the First Floor Back,* the most daring and audacious experiment ever made in the history of drama.' The following week Jerome K Jerome was correctly given credit for writing it. Forbes Robertson played the lead.

A grand wrestling match was held in December between Andrew Moyes of the Glasgow City Police and Andrew Rae of Dunfermline Police. This was followed by the annual pantomime with a complete ballet of continental dancers from The Folies Bergieres in Paris and The Casino Brussels.

Life wasn't all beer and skittles. The growth in number of emigration agents in Fife villages gives an indication of how far from content people were. Over the next few years, advertisements appeared for farm and factory hands and domestic workers for Canada, Australia and South Africa.

As early as 1911, people were aware of the possibility of war. In March, there was a great animated entertainment depicting life in the army and navy and explaining what would happen at the Call To Arms.

War was forgotten for a time in June with the coronation of George V. The Carnegie Dunfermline Trust held a coronation gala in Pittencrieff Park.

The Olympia Picture Palace opened in Canmore Street with a mixed bill of films and variety which included a one legged dancer and little Dollie du Barrie, the female Harry Lauder.

Flanagan & Allen

CHAPTER TWO

JOHN HENRY HARE

In May 1911, Potts relinquished his lease of the theatre. Bought by John Henry Hare in July 1912, the Opera House remained unused till January 1913, when it re-opened after having been reconstructed at great expense.

Hare, who came from a theatrical background, used his middle name to distinguish himself from another unrelated John Hare, a famous actor manager. Born in Dublin and educated at the University there, John Henry planned a career in medicine but after he was successful in early amateur stage performances the theatre proved irresistible.

He spent some time in Australia during the gold rush, then returned to London and the professional stage. He played all kinds of parts in touring companies in England and America and is said to have been in the original cast of *Charlie's Aunt*. He formed his own company touring the English provinces, and later brought it to Dunfermline.

Over the years, a number of writers have assumed that John Henry was a brother of the English actor Robertson Hare and possibly even of Doris Hare of *On The Buses* fame. In fact, he was related to neither. He had two brothers, James who owned the County Theatre in Bangor and moved into the cinema business, and Lumsden who became a top Hollywood actor.

Despite his Irish background, Lumsden played the typical British gentleman, military officer, doctor or lawyer, making his screen debut as F. Lums-

den Hare in 1916. Lumsden, who took his mother's maiden name, played the Prince Regent in *The House of Rothschild* (1934) and the King of Sweden in *Cardinal Richelieu* (1935).

One of those who made the successful transition from silent to talking films, he appeared in hundreds of film and television roles until his retirement in 1960.

Hare set a high standard for the class of companies he engaged for what was now The New Opera House, and his reconstruction of the theatre resulted in its becoming one of the best equipped and most up to date in Scotland.

The re-opening was announced on the first of January, with stalls costing one and sixpence and the gallery seats four pence. The opening show on the twentieth was *Aladdin*, the Williams' Company's eighth pantomime.

Prior to the raising of the curtain, Provost Husband and Mr Hare appeared before the footlights. The Provost said that he found his first appearance on stage rather disconcerting but was attending the opening ceremony to fulfil a promise made to Mr Hare.

In the two years since its last performance the theatre had undergone a transformation and a great deal of money had been spent to improve the building, including those parts behind the scenes.

The Provost wished Mr Hare good luck with his venture. Dunfermline, he said, with a population of thirty thousand people, was linked to the surrounding villages by tramways and if Hare kept his promise to bring good companies, the theatre would be well supported.

Drama was now fully recognised as an educative influence and Dunfermline should be ahead of other towns in the educational advantages it offered. Introducing Mr Hare, the Provost said that he fulfilled the second requirement for a successful theatre, namely good management. Hare had considerable experience in theatre management and had come to live in Dunfermline so he could personally supervise the business.

Mr Hare said that it had taken a tremendous effort to have the building ready for the opening that night. Construction had been hampered by a navvies' strike, but he wanted to express his gratitude to 'the humblest navvy who carried a hod' as well as to the architects and contractors.

A special word of thanks was due to Mr Cameron, the Superintendent of Works, who for some time had worked day and night to get the project finished on time.

His creed, Hare went on, was extremely simple. He would not use flamboyant advertisements or gifts to charity to encourage patrons, but would simply give them value for money, and a comfortable house, well lit and well warmed.

The performance of the pantomime was not without its problems. Mrs Williams asked that the audience would overlook the few hitches which had occurred. That morning, she had thought that there would be no possibility of the show going on that night, but in her line of business, apparently nothing was impossible.

Mrs Williams said that as a theatre-owner, she could say, unhesitatingly, that Dunfermline was one of the best in the country.

The local theatre critic was not entirely complimentary. Though the pantomime was successful with the singing above average, he felt that the cast appeared to be in want of a rehearsal. Nevertheless, the first night went remarkably smoothly and the dresses, magnificent scenery and electrical effects generally compared well to what he had seen in larger towns.

John Henry Hare

There was a humorous element supplied by Noel and Joel in a funny Hebrew patter and acrobatic act. 'Attractive items' were performed by The Sunshine Troupe of Dancers and other dance companies. The review ended with congratulations to Mr Hare on re-opening the theatre with such an excellent production.

One of Hare's early offerings was *The Cattle Thief*, 'a tale of Wyoming with real American bronchos, Indian ponies and a full brass band of American cowboys.' *Scenes from Wild Australia* used 'not actors but real bush men and women who handle snakes and crocodiles as if they were pet dogs; sharp shooters, bucking ponies and mules.' Patrons were offered a pound to stay on a mule for one whole minute.

Over the next weeks, the audience enjoyed an elephant wire walking act, pantomime, comedy and melodrama, including *The Chocolate Soldier and East Lynne. Bunty Pulls The Strings,* by Graham Moffatt, came direct from a successful run in The Haymarket Theatre in London; and *What Women Do for Love* was described as the latest coal mine sensation drama.

The theatre was already attracting overseas acts such as The Canadian Comedy Four, while plays and sketches covered a wide range of subjects. The *Panel Doctor* was described as a political skit; *The Ragged Patriot* as an episode in the life of a King's Messenger.

The messenger was an official of the Foreign Office whose duty it was to carry personally confidential messages from London to any embassy or legation abroad. His badge of office was a silver greyhound, and he was allowed to pass unchal

lenged through Customs with his 'diplomatic' bag.

In October 1913, a note of patriotism crept in with *Support Home Industries*. On the bill were Downs & Langford; A Military Miss; Walter Ellis and Company who performed *The Sleepwalker* and Hynd's *Comedy and Mystic Roosters.*

According to the newspaper report, Colin Hynd had been born and reared in Crossgates and trained his roosters there, and 'this troupe of birds has since attained a considerable measure of success in various provincial variety theatres.'

A new manager, James Fotheringham, had been appointed in August but there was no change in programming. Drama and variety appeared on the same bill, with no separation between straight plays and music hall items.

Novelty acts included Jerome and Jerome, patter and burlesque boxing comedians, and Darracq, a certified aviator, inventor of the sensation of the century - a car and driver whirled round a wheel at thirty miles an hour.

Mamselle Dalmere presented her table circus with performing rabbits, cat, dogs, doves, rats and monkeys. Rosa Hamel was an ambidextrous crayon impressionist.

Novelty jumping cyclists, sand and big boot dancers, mystic necromancers and aquatic acrobats vied with society gymnasts, and a race between an American motor car and a full blooded Mexican mustang.

Money may have been tight, because in April 1914, Hare formed Dunfermline Entertainments Ltd with a capital investment of one thousand pounds. The shareholders were his brother, James Hare, owner of the New County Theatre in Bangor, and Violet Verity from London. The company was never floated and in August, it was wound up.

A letter to The Edinburgh Gazette in September that year, headed New Opera House, describes the operation as 'a modern theatre complete in every detail; tip-up seats throughout with the exception of the gallery; own electric plant, 110 volts; the only dramatic house in West Fife; the population of the city is thirty five thousand and the enormous outside district linked up by electric cars. The immense new naval base at Rosyth is within the burgh boundaries.' This was probably a standard letter heading for correspondence with prospective acts because a footnote says that 'Any offer contained in this memo does not constitute a contract.'

Altogether, 1914 was a year of change. In January a talk on The Insurance Act was held in The Masonic Hall. The play *Saved by Wireless* used Marconi wireless instruments as used in battleships and cruisers and 'exactly similar to those used on the Titanic and Volturno.'

In August, to suit the military who were now in Dunfermline, the Opera House was to play twice every evening. By arrangement with Pathe Fieres and Central News Agency London, the latest war news and pictures were to be screened nightly.

It was possible learn to shoot at The Olympia Rifle range, see a film about The Fife and Forfarshire Yeomanry, buy flags in aid of the Red Cross or the Belgian Relief Fund - by 1915 there were over ten thousand Belgian refugees in Scotland - or watch *A Mill Girls Secret or The German Spy*. There were newspaper appeals for recruits for a new reserve battalion of the Argyll and Sutherland Highlanders.

By the beginning of the First World war, programmes begin to include names which are still familiar to us today. Florrie Forde brought her pantomime *Red Riding Hood*, and Harry Gordon, billed as a humorist, appeared with Fred Collins' Bohemian Entertainers. Gordon had made his Dunfermline debut at St Margaret's Hall in December 1911.

Born in Aberdeen in 1893, Harry Gordon was a comedian and pantomime dame. After appearing in talent contests at the Beach Pavilion, Aberdeen, when he was fifteen, he joined a pierrot troupe in Banchory where he met his future wife, Jessie Dudgeon.

She appeared as the Highland dancer Jose Goray, and they subsequently toured as the Two Elmas. There followed pre and first World War seasons in Aberdeen, Stonehaven and Burntisland during which time he met Jack Holden, who became his most accomplished stage partner and comic 'feed' for the rest of his career. Gordon introduced troupes of dancing girls and in his act portrayed over two hundred characters - including the Laird of Inversnecky.

Gordon was an artist, film maker and pioneer of radio, making broadcasts from The Beach Pavilion in Aberdeen; achieved a record of eleven years in pantomime at the Glasgow Alhambra, and ran summer shows at the Beach Pavilion in Aberdeen and in his act portrayed over two hundred characters - including the Laird of Inversnecky.

An artist, film maker and pioneer of radio, making broadcasts from The Beach Pavilion in Aberdeen, Gordon achieved a record of eleven years in pantomime at the Glasgow Alhambra, and ran summer shows at the Beach Pavilion in Aberdeen

From 1924 until 1940. He played seasons in Glasgow and Edinburgh in *Half-Past Eight*, toured Scotland and overseas, including Canada, America and South Africa; and from 1937, also appeared in the Alhambra, Glasgow pantomimes for sixteen years.

On the bill with Harry was Jack Holden and Jim Max, described as 'the immaculate coon' - no political correctness in those days.

Harry Gordon

What Would You Do? was said to deal with an everyday sex problem in an outspoken and fearless manner, but one of the four characters was a butler, so maybe not all that everyday. The programme also featured The Alabama Four, a coloured male quartet and J.J. Mannin, 'the coffee coloured coon.' *Now We Know* offered a backward glance into the days of Adam with thirty beauteous bathing belles.

Performances were topical. Poole's Myriorama, direct from The Synod Hall in Edinburgh presented tableaux and 'paintings' of the sinking of SS Kaiser Wilhelm and the charge of the Kilties and Scots Greys at St Quentin, plus 'a grand patriotic spectacle - *Britannia's Revue* illustrating Britain's call to arms.'

Battalion concerts were given by members of The Glasgow Highlanders and concerts in aid of Christmas comforts for men at the front.

Charles Windermere's advert for *Grumpy* in November 1915 asked the public to note that male members of his cast were not eligible for military service. This was important at a time when feelings ran high and white feathers were presented to men who appeared fit and healthy but were not in uniform.

Oor Wullie, the comedian W.W. Frame, with his songs and sayings, also gave an account of his experiences of the war in France.

The war did not halt the stream of odd characters like the Urma Sisters, trapeze artists, described as a pretty pair of suspenders; Madame Mizuah and her weird and wonderful mental telepathic séance, Russian singers and dancers and an Irish theatre.

For the first time, a photo of the star of the show appeared on the front page. Joe O' Gorman, with Harry Tate and Wal Pink, presented *Irish and Proud of It,* boasting a cast of fifty, new songs and new dresses. All received glowing reviews.

If theatre programmes were not to your taste, you could experience *A Trip To West Africa and Ceylon* courtesy of the co-operative lantern lectures or attend an exhibition of artificial flowers made by blind and cripple girls. Halley's comet had recently made its periodic visit and at least two acts had picked up on the name. In December 1916, *Haley's Komets* promised a performance of exceptional brilliancy.

People needed something to divert them from the grimness of every day living. Offices were opened for families to send parcels to soldiers at the front. Food was scarce. The Carnegie Trust organised meetings to instruct and encourage people in the cultivation of unused gardens and wasteland. This waste ground was divided up and the idea of allotments, as we know them today, was born.

There seemed to be no scarcity of weird and wonderful entertainers queueing up to perform in Dunfermline –acts like The Mafusiang Troupe of Chinese Wonders, the demon professor who swallowed chairs and tables and The Keystones, described as 'The Original Freak Wheel Inventors in a cyclonic, whimsical wheeling performance.'

A new play *Keep The Home Fires Burning* opened in May 1917 and Mackenzie Murdoch, the famous violinist came direct from his engagement with Harry Lauder. Other plays fitted into the spaces between Walton and Lester, the world's worst wizards, Hiawatha and Squaw with the most marvellous educated chimps ever presented on the vaudeville stage and Fidello who 'outrivalled Charlie Chaplin on the fiddle.'

Not the least of the stars to appear that year was the great Doctor Bodie, a very popular and flamboyant character who was either the most remarkable man on earth, a great healer and miracle worker, or a blatant charlatan. Plain Sam Bodie or perhaps even plainer Sam Murphy, he owed his reputation to his knowledge of electricity, having been an apprentice with the National Telephone Company.

At the beginning of the twentieth century few people knew about electricity and many remarkable claims were made for it. Bodie made his professional debut as a conjuror and ventriloquist, having acquired a name from his brother-in-law, and a dubious degree from America.

Not everyone took him at face value. Glasgow medical students complained about him in the press and greeted his appearance on stage by shouting 'Fake' and other stronger terms. The fire curtain was brought down, the students attacked the stage and were later fined 'derisory amounts.' Bodie claimed in the witness box that the letters MD after his name stood for 'Merry Devil.'

For the 'great doctor' it was good publicity. People flocked to see him, in Dunfermline as in other places. He appeared in The Alhambra and in St Margaret's Hall as well as the Opera House.

Using what he called 'hypnotism, Bodie force and bloodless surgery' he claimed to have treated hundreds of cases of paralysis during his career, and displayed a selection of discarded crutches outside theatres as proof.

Assisted by his wife, Princess Rubie, his 'electric magnetic' act kept him at the top of the bill in Britain and America for over forty years. His sister Marie Walford was known as Mystic Marie, Dr Bodie's real Trilby.

One of Bodie's oddest productions was *The Merry Monarch* or *Nell Gwynne's Haunted Boudoir*, which he brought to Dunfermline in January 1922. It was advertised as the first ever Historical Ventriloquial Comedy Drama. It was probably also the last.

In 1917, Bodie called himself 'The Hero of the Arabia.' His company was said to be made up of survivors of the ill fated RMS Arabia, sunk by a German submarine on their way home from a successful tour of South Africa, India, Ceylon and The Far East.

Bodie demonstrated his famous cage of death, the death chair and a submarine searchlight, invented by him and presented to the Admiralty. He claimed to pass thirty thousand volts through his body and even wrote the songs for the show.

On occasion, the theatre was given free for organisations raising money for prisoners of war food funds and other war charities. Many touring companies must have been made up of rather elderly gentlemen but as men were discharged or invalided out, they rejoined the troupe.

All had to be registered ineligible for service and one wonders what they felt about *In The Trenches,* said to be a screaming comedy sketch whose setting could be '*any old trench.'*

November 1917 saw the first visit of Marie Kendall, famous for her song '*Just Like The Ivy'* which she sang throughout America, Australia and South Africa. Born in 1873, she made her first stage appearance at the age of five and played melodramatic child roles for the next ten years before going on to pantomime and music hall. She is said to be the first and only woman to play seven halls in London every night for a month.

Marie Kendall appeared in the Royal Variety Show at the London Palladium in 1932 and though she retired in 1939, continued to make occasional appearances till her death at the age of ninety one.

Marie Kendall

On the bill with Miss Kendall was Florence Smithson who presented The Eight Jolly Sailors. They are described as the eight Jutland Boys, bright, breezy, buoyant boys from the North Sea battles in an entertaining comedy scene.

Other acts included comedian Gus Keeling; Billie Chester, described as the girl with a glorious voice; Gino the boy musician; Phil Bransby, the London comedian with his cockney characters; Franco's Midgets; and Helen Charles, entertainer and raconteur.

1918 was a bad year. A new railway station was opened at Rosyth to serve the dockyard. The Fifeshire Food Control Committee was in charge of rationing and protest meetings were held against what was seen as profiteering. Speakers included representatives from the miners' unions and the co-operative society. Butter, margarine, tea and meat were in short supply. Restaurants could only open at allotted times and if customers wanted sugar in their tea, they had to supply it themselves. Women were to be trained to work in the munitions industry at the Fife Mining School in Cowdenbeath. Farmers were advised to start growing flax before compulsory orders were issued.

Meanwhile, *The Khaki Boys,* back from the front, wounded and discharged provided an alfresco entertainment. Prohibitionists invited people to hear what prohibition had done for Canada and America; Lord John Sanger brought his musical sea lions and Gordon Brown, 'The Beau Brummel of the Variety Stage' strutted his stuff. John Henry Hare expanded his empire, taking over the Olympia with Ernest Cooper as manager. Films and variety ran side by side in both theatres.

The Armistice didn't make it to the front page but there were notices of services of thanksgiving in many of the churches. The 1918 Representation of the People Act had given women the vote for the first time and the Liberal Association held its first meeting of members and voters of both sexes to choose a new parliamentary candidate.

After the election, the expense account of all candidates was printed in full. A testimonial was to be given for Sergeant David Ferguson Hunter, VC, from Dunfermline, and a special treat in The Palace Kinema for 'the children of the poorer classes in the City to celebrate the signing of the armistice.'

Fred Karno was at The Olympia with his *Mumming Birds*. In the Opera House *Over The Top*, a melodramatic musical revue in eight scenes featured ' a host of wounded and discharged soldiers who have recently returned from France, and having done their bit, will take part in a most realistic battle, *The Fight for Bagdad*. German spies and their plots are revealed in the cellar scene.'

The first years of peace remained grim. Guns, munitions and captured trophies were displayed in St Catherine's Wynd. Restrictions on the sale of cream and jam were removed but sugar, tea and meat were still rationed. Parents were urged to give children sugar and make do themselves with saccharine.

Meetings were held to demand pensions for soldiers and sailors, and appeals made for money to build war memorials. The Ministry of Munitions started selling off huts and building materials, ranges, baths and boilers from their depots in North Queensferry, Rosyth and Crombie. In April 1921, a concert and film show was held in aid of the Miners' Distress Fund.

In the world of make believe, Dr Bodie was giving 'the greatest exposition of ventriloquism the world has ever seen.' A season of Shakespeare, Sheridan and Goldsmith was presented by The Compton Comedy Company, This was very much a family affair. Edward Compton ran the company for over thirty years, his wife took over when he died and the cast contained two of their daughters.

A new play *Dope*, claimed to deal with the greatest evil of the present day - which surely proves that's nothing is new. Fred Karno returned with *Kill or Kure.* Basically, the programme was the mixture as before - plays direct from London theatres, occasional drama but mostly light comedy, revues and novelty acts.

The popularity of the theatre was no doubt helped by the local transport companies. Special buses were arranged for patrons from Kelty on Wednesdays, and Culross on Wednesdays and Saturdays.

Tram cars to Cowdenbeath and Rosyth waited till the end of the show, and special late trams ran to Kelty and Lochgelly on Wednesday evenings. The theatre also benefited from professional managers with a wide knowledge of the entertainments business.

Clockwise from top left – Jack Holden, Tommy Yorke, Sandy Daw, and Tommy Morgan

CHAPTER THREE

THE GOLDEN YEARS

From 1919 the theatre was under the management of a Mr Buchanan, who had been appointed resident manager by Hare.

A Dunfermline business man, whose father had been manager of professional touring and dramatic companies, Buchanan was in his younger days associated with the management of travelling entertainment companies.

In May 1920, the Opera House closed for redecoration and refurbishment. Hare continued running the Olympia with its seemingly endless stream of burlesque novelties and vocal acts, including Belle Sylvia, Scotland's leading baritone and the strangely titled 'Four Wotucaulems.' Among the other acts were Will Fyffe, Lily Morris and Lucan and McShane.

Arthur McShane was born in Lancashire in 1887 and began his stage career in variety and concert parties. In 1912 he played his first dame, an old Irish washerwoman by the name of Mrs O'Flynn. The next year he married sixteen year old Kitty and they toured Ireland with a mother and daughter act, based on the old washerwoman, which eventually became *Old Mother Riley and her Daughter Kitty.*

They were phenomenally successful, appeared at the London Palladium, starred in radio, stage and pantomime and made fourteen films.

Unfortunately, their marriage was a stormy affair and their antics on screen were a tame version of what went on off stage. Lucan's last film, without his wife, was *Mother Riley Meets the Vampire,* starring Bela Lugosa. At the height of their career, Lucan and McShane were said to be earning a thousand pounds a week.

The refurbishment carried out on the building at this time was extremely important. The remodelling of the interior, at a time when few theatres were being built in Britain, resulted in an unusually fine auditorium containing the features which would make it such an attractive proposition to the Americans more than sixty years later.

Roy Jackson's original design had two balconies supported on iron columns, stage boxes and a domed ceiling. The new design provided cantilevered balconies and completely changed the form of the ceiling, the boxes and the proscenium arch.

The decorative plasterwork was now in a Louis XV style and the twenty four foot wide proscenium set within a deep arched reveal. The fly tower was raised and the wing space of the stage increased.

The theatre was to re-open on August 1st, 1921 and the Dunfermline Press reported that 'after a somewhat lengthy period of closure, the Opera House with the word Hippodrome added to its title is now nearing time when it will be reopened to the public.'

In fact it had been The Opera House and Hippodrome since May 1913, when it was host to Mannon's Maniac Mummies.

Now, for some reason, the titles were reversed.

'Extensive alterations and improvements have been carried out,' the report continues, 'and we may venture to suggest that the Opera House will one day rank as one of the handsomest and most up to date entertainment houses of its kind in the country.

No expense has been spared and every conceivable detail which could further the comfortable accommodation of the public has been attended to.

The entrance hall, previously done in paper has been handsomely finished in oak panelling into which background has been set four tapestried panels. The hall has been lengthened and access to the body of the theatre is now much simpler, and less prone to cause congestion.'

The corridor and stairways were laid with new fire and vermin proof composition tiling, the walls were panelled and mirrors placed at a convenient points 'for the benefit of young ladies anxious to give a final touch to their headgear.'

The new scheme of decoration was 'most artistic with none of the loud and flashy colours so often seen.' Ceiling panels appeared in daylight as a 'sickly shade of heliotrope' but in artificial light became a rich warm mauve.

The ceiling was lit by nine bowl lights, and amber tinted globes with white shades adorned the tier fronts, contributing hugely to 'the rich effulgence which results from the full utilisation of the lighting system.'

Panels on the auditorium wall represented Shakespearian characters and the proscenium arch was strikingly decorated with fibrous plaster work.

The new Hippodrome was to be run chiefly as a variety theatre, but many leading theatrical companies were booked for the winter season. The opening performance featured Mr Fred Collins' Revue *Keep Guessing.*

One of the stars making his first appearance in Dunfermline that year in *The Disorderly Room* was Tommy Handley, later to be famous for the radio show *ITMA.* Handley served in the first war, mostly as a member of an army concert party, then toured with Jack Hylton, teaming up to form Handley and Hylton.

Their sketch, *The Disorderly Room*, written by Eric Blore, was a musical skit on an army court martial with dialogue set to popular tunes. It soon became an established favourite, and remained so for over twenty years.

Tommy Handley's first studio broadcast was in 1925 and ITMA, first heard in 1939 became the most popular programme of the war. The initials stood for *It's That Man Again* which was also the show's theme tune. It ran for over three hundred performances, and three days after the final broadcast in January 1949, Handley died at the age of fifty two.

A new comedy *Froth* included in its cast Tommy Lorne, later to be a staple of Scots entertainers. Born Hugh Gallagher Corcoran near Glasgow, as a boy he joined a local troupe, The Port Dundas Court Juvenile Minstrels, making his music hall debut in a George Formby Senior Talent competition at the Queen's Theatre, Glasgow.

After touring Scotland as the burlesque and dance act, Wallace and Lorne, he became principal comedian at the Princess Theatre, Glasgow in 1920.

Now an established solo performer, he developed his own comic style, with eccentric clownish make-up, a kilt, Glengarry bonnet, high collar with a bootlace tie, a short jacket, long white gloves and large boots.

In 1928 he played Dame for the first time at the King's Theatre, Edinburgh, launching a successful pantomime career. Among his professional admirers were Harry Gordon and Will Fyffe.

The range and quality of performers and performances is striking. In March 1922, the bill included Mario Lorenzo, Italian Harpist; Paul Freeman, card manipulator, the violinist Sylvestro and Lily Morrris.

A London comedienne, with a long career as a soubrette and as principal boy in pantomime, Lily went on to do a solo act and became famous for songs such as *Why am I Always the Bridesmaid?* and *Don't Have Any More, Missus Moore.*

August that year saw a production of the Sherlock Holmes mystery *The Speckled Band.* A musical comedy revue, *See You Later,* 'with eight scenes of laughs and screams' featured Renee Houston and Billie Benson.

Sisters from Renfrewshire, and born into a music hall family, they first appeared as a double act in 1920, before Renee went solo in revue and pantomime and later graduated to film and television roles.

She made a number of appearances in Dunfermline, the final one with her husband Donald Stewart. According to Andy Stewart, Renee gave Norman wisdom his first break, in the revue *Cockles and Champagne.*

Novelty acts and revues were popular and many were imported direct from their run in London theatres. A week of plays starring Sir J. Forbes Robertson included *The Passing of the Third Floor Back, Of Mice and Men, The Call of the Road* and *Rosemary.*

Pantomimes offered fun, frolic and frivolity as well as gorgeous scenery, magnificent costumes, stage and electrical effects. All this for sixpence if you wanted to sit in the balcony. The best stalls cost two shillings, four pence extra if reserved.

There was an election that year and John Wallace, the Liberal candidate addressed meetings of electors, but perhaps he was nervous of meeting the newly enfranchised women for he called on his wife to speak to them at a separate meeting. His tactics didn't work though and the Labour candidate won. Wallace was not happy and wrote to the press:

'At a time of acute industrial depression unequalled in our history a Socialist could make a strong appeal and specious promises impossible of fulfilment. The time of disillusionment will soon come. Personally I would rather retire from public life than promise what I can't perform ...'

Ah well, plus ca change ...

Charlie Kemble, who appeared with The Scottish Co-optimists in 1922, went on to hold two records, one for the number of venues he played in Dunfermline, the other for the longest continuous show which ran for fifty four weeks.

Another popular turn was Stanford and Allen, a double act which would later split up to form two other acts. Chesney Allen teamed up with Bud Flanagan and the rest is history. They were at one time part of Florrie Forde's company.

Florrie first appeared on stage in Sydney in 1893, and in London in 1897. She was a large buxom lady, who favoured costumes beautifully adorned with feathers and sequins, and became popular with her renditions of such pub songs as *Down at the Old Bull and Bush, Hold your Hand Out You Naughty Boy*. During the First World War, she delighted audiences with *It's a Long Way to Tipperary*.

Florrie Forde

Florrie toured Britain extensively, appearing as Principal Boy in dozens of pantomimes, even when she was sixty. At the start of the second World War, she entertained the troops with songs like *What's the Use of Worrying.*

Though she never appeared at the Opera House, Florrie's pantomimes did, and she arranged for members of her company, including Aleta Turner, *The Personality Girl,* to appear there. Jenny Lee, the politician, remembered Florrie staying in the Lee family's hotel in Lochgelly.

The artistes in *Hunky Dory* claimed to have played their parts at home and abroad over one thousand times. Meaning all right or in good condition, the title still exists in the everyday language of many Fife people.

If you didn't care for such things, *The Sheik*, starring Rodolph Valentino was in the Alhambra, but *On The Dole* was probably closer to people's experiences. The Carnegie Trust Drama Class presented *Trelawney of the Wells*, and special mention was made of local merchant, William Hodes, who supplied the chandelier and all the furnishings.

The D'Oyly Carte Company did a season of Gilbert and Sullivan in the Alhambra shortly before it closed as a theatre. It reopened in August 1924 as The Temple of the Motion Picture.

The winter season at the Opera House opened with *The Officers' Mess,* boasting a cast including bathing girls, river girls, pyjama girls and jewel girls. The theatre now had a licensed and refreshment bar on the circle floor.

In September, the Headwell Bowling Green was opened with the Provost's wife throwing the first jack.

You could go for an evening tram-bus tour round Loch Leven or to Rumbling Bridge, or the more fortunate could take a trip by sea to London for a mere eight guineas.

The Christmas holiday production for 1924, *Scotch Broth,* a 'palatable and pleasing concoction,' introduced Dave Willis, a new comic. Born in Glasgow, he first appeared on stage as a child, assisting his brother Claude, a conjuror, at the Panopticon and other Glasgow theatres.

At thirteen, he appeared in the Theatre Royal chorus in pantomime, while beginning an engineering apprenticeship. After the First World War, he gained experience in amateur concert-parties and worked regularly in cine-variety in the west of Scotland.

The early thirties saw him in pantomime at the Theatre Royal and Pavilion, and he developed his unique clowning humour, starring in *Half-Past Eight* and pantomimes in Edinburgh and Glasgow.

A small man with a toothbrush moustache, his looks and his talent led Willis to be nicknamed the Charlie Chaplin of Scotland. Particularly popular during the War, his famous character sketches included Hitler.

According to Gordon Irving, his impression of the Fuhrer at the time of the Munich crisis came to the notice of the Nazis. They complained to the Foreign Office and Lord Inverclyde was sent to ask him to desist. Other impressions included Gandhi.

One of his catch phrases 'Way, way up a kye', came from his small son. Dave was in The Royal Flying Corps and whenever the young Willis saw an aeroplane he would say 'That's my Daddy, way, way up a kye.'

Dave retired in 1951 but later returned to the stage, touring throughout Scotland, including a visit to the Carnegie Hall in 1955, and continued working until late in life. Beryl Reid remembered working with him. He looked comic, she said, with legs too short and arms too long but he had a touch of genius about him.

Together they did over four hundred sketches, none of which were written down, everything was ad libbed.

An otherwise uninspiring year's programme opened with a visit from Mrs Patrick Campbell, who was an enormous star. Born Beatrice Tanner in 1865, she was unusual in being known by her husband's name.

She married at nineteen, began her stage career four years later, leapt to fame in *The Second Mrs Tanqueray* and was still unbeatable in to the role when she came to Dunfermline in 1925.

Her Shakespearian roles included Juliet and Lady Macbeth. Mrs Campbell had a long friendship with George Bernard Shaw and the part of Eliza Doolittle in *Pygmalion* was specially written for her.

In The Cinema in East Port patrons could share in *Plastigrams,* described as 'the screen's greatest joke.' In an early form of three dimensional viewing, characters could 'leave the screen and march slap-bang among the audience.' Free plastigram spectacles were provided to help make this possible.

The only front page indication of the misery endemic in the coal mining areas in 1926 is the notice of emergency regulations concerning the supply of coal.

Light comedies and revues with the occasional 'serious' play filled the bills. With the development of talking films, 'a new and novel entertainment' in 1927 included film tests to discover the ideal film face in the audience.

Comedian Lex McLean was a new name, at the bottom of the list in a line up of Lyndon & Moore, Rab Ross, Tommy Dale, Bernard Granville, Bob Dundas and Archie Bentley.

While he was often described as 'earthy' and nicknamed 'Sexy Lexy', his material only had a touch of the *double entendre* and he filled the

Lex Mclean

Pavilion Theatre, Glasgow, the Tivoli, Aberdeen and the Palladium, Edinburgh, for many seasons during the fifties and sixties with family audiences.

Lex was a popular television entertainer with his own comedy series, in which he was regularly assisted by Walter Carr. Regarded as the last of the old-style music hall comedians, his death in 1975 was said to mark the end of the traditional summer variety season at the Pavilion.

Charlie Kemble introduced his new company of super entertainers - Jennie Collins, Mason Sisters, Tommy Dale, Dave Bruce, John Hilton, Willie Larmer, Jack Anthony, Maie Wynne - and there were *Special all Scotch Nights* on Thursdays and Fridays.

Of these entertainers, probably Jack Anthony became the best known. Born in Glasgow in 1900, John Anthony Herbertson was never known as anything other than Jack Anthony, a name that his father, also an entertainer, adopted in America. Jack began singing and dancing in Kinderspiels and charity concert parties in Glasgow.

Appearances in the Fyffe & Fyffe shows in Rothesay led to the Millport Entertainers in 1926 where he became a good all-rounder, a singer, dancer and comedian, often made-up with the white face and outsize clothes of a clown. He partnered G H. Elliot, *The Chocolate Coloured Coon,* at the Pavilion. His comic feeds were Bertha Ricardo and, from 1929, Bond Rowell.

The Laureate Players had a ten week run of plays ranging from *The Importance of Being Earnest* to *The Unfair Sex* but audiences did not turn out just for the big show business names.

Home grown talent was well supported. Joe Corrie and his Fife Players with *Time o Strife* were a welcome change from the mostly frothy offerings of London companies. Most of Corrie's plays were performed in Dunfermline and, as the press reported in September 1929:

'No introduction is required in a notice of this week's show at the Opera house. The mere statement that Corrie's Fife Players were appearing was sufficient.

Some people, who do not know the trials and difficulties in the mining villages, the insecurity of the miner's life, the strenuousness of his work, his tremendous struggle to make ends meet, would be pleased if only they could think that Corrie had overdrawn his picture by presenting a caricature.

Yet the picture is a true one. We may object to it on propaganda lines if we care, but at the same time we have got to realise that trade unionism and politics, especially discussion on the communist and labour parties, are as vital to the miner as a shave or his breakfast. The miner says what he means. There are no smart alecs among the miners.

The two redeeming features of the whole pitiful business is first the fact that under their rough exterior, there is a heart of gold and a mind as humble as a child's.

The second is their extraordinary unselfishness. Their womenfolk would share their last shilling to help a neighbour who is carrying a greater burden than themselves.

In the play *Time o Strife* we have a portion of history we cannot forget. The company at the Opera House this week is the same talented one that visited Dunfermline in May last year.'

Another home grown talent who had made it internationally was Will Fyffe. Born in Dundee in 1885, he joined his father's company of barnstormers, so called because they travelled around the country playing in barns or wherever they could set up their show.

His first role was little Willie in *East Lynne* and gained so much experience that by the time he was fifteen, he was playing Polonius in *Hamlet*.

When Harry Lauder and Neil Kenyon turned down some sketches he'd written, Fyffe decided to work them himself and toured with variety shows , making his first music hall appearance in London in 1916.

After thirty years on the stage, he became an overnight success as a music hall comedian and made his first of four appearances in Royal Command performances in 1922.

He was a character actor rather than a comedian, using his own sketches and inventions - an old shepherd, a poacher, railway guard and ship's engineer. His village idiot, *Daft Sandy* was described as a masterpiece of tragi-comedy.

I Belong to Glasgow and *Sailing up the Clyde* remain popular today. Fyffe toured America, was a regular broadcaster, made many films and was awarded a CBE for his work during the Second World War. He died in 1947.

For his 1929 Dunfermline show, Will was advertised a 'the attraction of the year' and the paper was unstinting in its praise :

'In these days of mechanised entertainment it is refreshing to come upon one who in spite of the deluge of Americanism that seems to have descended on us, can hold the stage for the best part of an hour. Will Fyffe is a Scot and one who has gained honour in his chosen profession both home and abroad, with a royal command performance, and a newspaper leader devoted to him.

Entitled *The Art of Will Fyffe* it appeared in the Montreal 'Daily World' on the comedian's first visit to that city and said he was 'one of the outstanding exponents of vaudeville today.

The secret of his success lies in the completeness and sympathy with which he presents each

study, seeming to get right under the surface of the character to bring to light all that is lovable and humorous.

He is to present two new studies *Dr MacGregor Sailing up the Clyde* and *The Centenarian* in addition to those which have brought him fame.'

One of Will's supporting acts was Coram the celebrated ventriloquist. With his dummy Jerry, he had just returned from a world tour having presented his *Whitehall* scene in practically every English speaking country in the world.

Among the alternative sources of entertainment was *An Exhibition of a Film* held in the Palace Kinema and provided by the British Social Hygiene Council. One may hazard a guess at the contents for only adults over eighteen were cordially invited to attend.

In February 1930 Dunfermline United Burns Club held its one hundred and fourteenth anniversary dinner. The Opera house was showing *Just a Minute* and no doubt women would be able to attend if they could spare a minute from their household duties.

According to an advert for Burns and Glen, Italian Warehousemen, they could supply such necessities as Spanish whiting, crocus powder - nothing to do with the flower, it was a kind of red or yellow metal polish - scrubbers, switches, hearth brooms, pipe clay and housemaids gloves.

They were also offering whisky by the gallon as well as by the bottle and suggesting Australian burgundy as a pick-me-up after flu.

Will Fyffe

A new Miners Institute was to be built in Kinglassie and for ladies only, there was a free lecture and demonstration by The Dreadnought School of Dresscutting.

The London Symphony Orchestra were playing in St Margaret's Hall and Charlie Kemble's Entertainers included Jack Anthony and Alec Finlay. A comic actor and singer, Finlay was born in 1906, and was a child singer of Lauder songs at charity concert parties.

Known as 'The Pocket Harry Lauder', he made his professional debut in Millport in 1928, formed a double act with his wife Rita Andre, and first appeared in London in 1931. They toured Britain and South Africa, returning to Scotland in the late thirties, when Alec began his 'Scotland's Gentleman' act, wearing top hat, tail coat and kilt.

An accomplished musician, Finlay also became a successful all-round entertainer, often performing in pantomime with Harry Gordon, and in revue, as a character actor known for his portrayal as the Wee Free Kirk elder.

Will Fyffe, with Torrani the Singing Puzzle and the Seven Midget Gladiators, had strong competition from the increasing lure of the picture house with attractions like *All Quiet on the Western Front*, Charlie Chaplin and Laurel and Hardy.

In May 1931, therefore, Hare applied successfully for permission to make alterations to facilitate the introduction of talkies and in August the theatre saw yet another opening, this time with a mixture of talkies and variety.

In his welcoming speech, Hare said that there might be regrets that the older human type of entertainment was being discontinued but it was obvious to all managers of theatres outside large cities that an adequate supply of first rate dramatic attractions could no longer be relied on for every week of the season. He would still try, from time to time, to book some of the excellent companies that were available.

In the first week, the new style of entertainment attracted large audiences. The British Thomson-Houston system of reproduction had proved a complete success and the fare offered was excellent. The acoustics of the theatre were admirably suited to this form of entertainment.

The first 'talkie' shown, *Just Imagine*, proved most entertaining with a glimpse fifty years into the future. A trip to Mars in a projectile shot from the earth was the outstanding incident in the story and 'some highly amusing scenes' took place on the planet. The show contained both live and screen performances as the newspaper reports: 'The variety part of the entertainment is provided by the Godwin Four, who appear on the stage in a musical cabaret act in which they introduce violin and cello playing, singing and dancing.'

The next week it was John Wayne and Tyrone Power in *The Big Trail* and, within a short time, the live entertainment was dropped and continuous showing of films introduced.

Although Hare's reconstruction of the theatre resulted in its becoming one of the best equipped and most up to date in Scotland, this venture into the movie business was not a financial success. Picture houses opened everywhere. People living in Rosyth, Inverkeithing and Newmills for example, now had no need to travel. They had films on their own doorsteps.

Dance halls were also springing up in most Fife villages.

The Opera House still hosted live entertainment from time to time. In February, a grand concert was held in aid of the Police Boot and Clothing Fund for Necessitous Children.

Concert parties still brought stars like Bobby Howard, Jack Anthony and Tommy Lorne. Edward Dunstan and Company presented a season of Shakespeare plays.

In June the theatre closed for the summer vacation. It turned out to be a long one.

Shortly afterwards, on the eighteenth of June, theatre patrons were shocked to hear that the body of Hare, who had been the proprietor of The Opera House for nearly twenty years, had been found on the LNER Railway line near Kirkliston.

Hare, who had been to England on business, was returning home to Dunfermline when his death occurred.

Extract from Dunfermline City Chambers visitors' book

CHAPTER FOUR

THE THIRTIES

When John Henry Hare acquired the Opera House, he set a high standard for the class of companies he engaged and until industrial depression overtook Dunfermline and West Fife, the theatre had a reputation which was the envy of many Scottish provincial towns.

It is surprising then, that it was allowed to stay unused for almost two years before inquiries were made by a Glasgow law firm on behalf of clients wishing to obtain a licence to run the theatre for a year. In an interview in February 1934, Horace Collins of the Collins Variety Agency of Glasgow and Edinburgh, announced that the Opera House would reopen for four weeks from February 26.

The agency had been started by James Alfred Nelson, a master painter who, just after the Boer War, began making his name as a comedian. He changed his name to Fred Collins and as well as performing, became an agent and impresario. He set up the Collins Variety Agency in Glasgow and, with his son Horace, groomed many Scots stars of the twenties and thirties, and went on to take control of a number of theatres.

Collins' initial attraction in Dunfermline would be Harry Gordon, 'the famous wireless and variety comedian' who had just concluded a record pantomime season at the Theatre Royal Edinburgh and The Pavilion, Glasgow.

Harry was to present a road show type of entertainment called *Inversnecky Calling*. Sir Harry Lauder was also scheduled to appear in what was claimed would be the biggest theatrical event that the town had seen for many years.

A band of painters were engaged to redecorate the front of the house and powerful electric lights were installed underneath the canopy. The switchboard was doubled in size by the inclusion of several hundred extra lights and a new set of dimmers. Seats were vacuumed and the woodwork polished.

Under the watchful eye of Horace Collins, the theatre was prepared for the host of entertainers already booked to appear. As well as Harry Lauder, these included Dave Willis and Will Fyffe.

Sir Harry Lauder's visit took place on March 17th, 1934. On his arrival at the Opera House on the Monday, he was met by Provost McKay who accompanied him to the City Chambers where he signed the distinguished visitors book.

On the Wednesday he paid a visit with the Provost to the Dunfermline Silk Mills where he expressed his admiration for the fine fabrics produced.

At St Margaret's and Pilmuir Works, he was met by Angus Robertson, the joint chairman of directors. On a guided tour of the works, he spoke to girls at their looms, and at weaving and embroidering machines. In the warehouse, he 'made several humorous remarks which kept them in glee'.

Heads of department were presented to him and he had a cheery word of encouragement for everyone.

The line up with Sir Harry for his week's engagement at The Opera House included Grace Clarke and Colin Murray, popular piano entertainers. Billed as Scotland's Burns and Allen, they were a very successful team, he as the henpecked husband, she the hectoring wife.

She played, he sang and they were a musical and light comedy act for over twenty years before branching out into a broader type of sketch comedy. They were the first husband and wife team in Scotland to be awarded the BEM for services to entertainment.

The cost of admission for Sir Harry's show was higher than usual, probably in deference to his great reputation. Instead of stalls, circle, pit and gallery, seats were advertised as orchestra stalls, stalls, dress circle and gallery. The latter now cost a shilling.

Close on the heels of Sir Harry came the ever popular Will Fyffe, followed by Max Waldorf, later to become famous as Max Wall, and his Pack. The theatre then closed for the summer, with plans to reopen on August 24th.

According to the Press, The Opera House had proved a popular place of entertainment during the winter months, possibly because it was the only variety theatre in Fife, and this was taken to demonstrate that there was a demand locally for good vaudeville and theatre productions.

Top of the bill acts would be supported by several other outstanding artistes. New bookings included Bobby Telford and Company, Bert Denver's show, Tommy Morgan and Company, the Great Lavante, illusionist and George West, star of pantomime in Glasgow.

Most top comedians had their own specialities and West was an avid film fan who specialised in parodies of Shirley Temple, Mae West and WC Fields.

In August Charles Denville took over Opera House for an unspecified time. He had previously come for four weeks and was so successful that he stayed for a year. Now he was to open with the record breaking comedy, *Paddy, The Next Best Thing.*

Denville was the son of the Conservative MP for Newcastle who was one of the pioneers of the repertory movement and had been associated with the theatre since his youth. The Denville Famous Players had repertory companies in every large city in the United Kingdom and had successful runs in Dundee, Greenock and Paisley.

In an interview with the Dunfermline Journal, Denville said he was coming to Dunfermline for no set period, and the length of his stay depended on the support he received from the local theatre going public. He hoped to take over the whole concern and provide a permanent theatre in Dunfermline.

Paddy was perhaps the best known and most popular comedy on the stage at the time. Originally produced at the Savoy Theatre in London in 1930, it played to over a million people in the next four years and when it went to the provinces as many as five companies were touring it at the same time.

Denville's company were offering two shows a night when one was normal. This was done by cutting interval times but not the script.

Prices were to be kept down, something of 'considerable importance in these times of stringency,' and this was obviously successful because the company had a twenty week run of plays from August to December 1934 .

1935 began with the usual pantomime, and the New International Zoo Circus which boasted the only lion in the world to fire a gun, a boxing pony, and performing horses , dogs and mules.

Professor John Popjie, the Dutch Savant introduced *The Great Radiana* which could shave a man, do conjuring tricks, bake a cake, sing popular songs and play the piano. One thousand pounds reward was offered to anyone who could explain how this marvel worked.

An aptly named Stromboli performed a 'most remarkable fire act', while Wilfred Briton, the ninth wonder of the world, could break iron bars, lift a piano and the pianist, and pull ten ton trucks with his teeth.

Other more intriguing acts followed, among them *Bithells Wonder Crows*, the only performing crows in the world, and *Lester's American Midget Circus* which advertised their midgets as 'real living gnomes' who had toured America and had seasons in New York, Paris and London.

They performed *Cinderella* and were accompanied by a special augmented orchestra and midget opera.

Kentucky Days, presented as The Great American Broadcasting Revue, boasted the world famous American minstrels, past masters in the art of black faced minstrelsy.

Dancing girls were always a feature. In 1922 it was The Waverley Girls and The Unity Troupe of Dancers, then came The Four Saxon Girls who did taps and tempo; The Ten Flexees; The Ten Morganettes, who later increased to Fourteen; The Meltonian Girls; The Ten Joy Girls and The Saronies .

The Texas Cliffe Trio were 'Those Hot Chocolate Steppers 'and in 1937 there were Ten John Tiller Girls and twelve Winstanley Rosebuds.

Then there were The Dryburgh Girls, led by Grace, the wife of Lex McLean and last but not least The Moxon Girls or The Moxon Ladies as they were sometimes known - of whom, more later.

By August 1935 though, the theatre was again under new management and according to the Press, patrons would hardly recognise it. Another make over had changed the colour scheme to marigold with bands of brilliant scarlet, iridescent green and gold. The decorative plaster work round the proscenium arch was picked out with a repetition of marigold, green and gold shades.

The report said that 'last year the theatre was acquired by a local company who aim to provide the best class of entertainment in variety, musical comedy and of course pantomime.

The theatre will open with the great London musical comedy success *'Mr Cinders'* and will be followed by artistes of high repute.'

The new company was The Opera House Dunfermline Company whose Director and resident manager was J F.O'Driscoll. The other shareholders were John and Daniel Fraser, both Dunfermline business men, and William Burt who was described as a Doctor of Philosophy.

O'Driscoll had a great deal of experience, had been involved in the construction of the Royalty

Kinema, Dundee; was manager of The Palace, Rothesay for four years and of The Plaza ballrooms there, and later manager of the Parkhead Picture Palace, Glasgow.

He saw service in France and Belgium in World War One where he organised concerts for troops. He boxed for the British army and was an inspector for the Scottish branch of The British Boxing Board of Control.

The Opera House was billed as Fife's only variety theatre, and the newspapers waxed lyrical about the fare offered by the newly refurbished building:

'A particularly fine attraction has been secured for the opening on September 9th. *Mr Cinders*, perhaps the brightest of modern musical comedies. The London Hippodrome success is admirably presented by Mr Victor Pierpoint and suffers much less than might be expected by its translation into a twice nightly show. The scene changing waits have been kept to a minimum.

Jim, the masculine equivalent of Cinderella, and Jill as his audacious and irrepressible fairy godmother, are the central figures in the play. Peter Miller and Eileen Hastings put any amount of vim as well as artistry into their presentation.

Eileen's role gives scope for her vivid sense of humour as well as the charm of her singing and the grace of her dancing.'

Top of the bill in September was Veronica, Dunfermline's own star, who achieved world wide fame as high kicking champion of the world. She was described as the girl with the two thousand pound legs. Also on the bill were Alec Finlay and Rita Andre, the Scottish new star comedy, Clarke and Murray and Gladys Church, the whistling songstress.

In December, Robert Wilson, then principal tenor with the D'Oyly Carte Opera Company performed at a concert in St Margaret's Hall.

Robert Wilson was born in Cambuslang and sang in a local choir before joining the Rothesay Entertainers in his early twenties. Having trained and toured with the D'Oyly Carte Opera Company for five years, he abandoned an operatic career to establish himself during the forties as the leading singer in revue.

Robert Wilson

Billed as 'The Voice of Scotland', his repertoire was a popular blend of light opera and Scottish ballads, such as *Down in the Glen* and *Here's to the Gordons*.

He appeared with Jack Anthony and Jack Radcliffe in road shows across Scotland, before managing his own touring companies in the early fifties, choosing comedians such as Stanley Baxter and Johnny Beattie, and often giving young entertainers their first break.

In the mid-fifties, he founded the White Heather Group which, during the following years, proved a training ground for young singers, including Andy Stewart, Sydney Devine and Joe Gordon.

1936 began with Wendy Wood, the self styled 'Scottish Patriot,' giving a talk in the Co-operative hall on her 'Vision of New Scotland' and Aneurin Bevan spoke on 'The Rise of the Modern State.'

The Pharmacy Act banned the sale to the general public except by licence of, among other things, mercury, formaldehyde, arsenic and sulphuric acid. The amount of poison readily available over the counter at that time is quite frightening

The death of George V was marked by appeal for funds for a memorial, and plans were made for a public dinner for older inhabitants of the town to celebrate the coronation of Edward VIII.

A ladies football match was held at East End Park - Mae Watson's Bowhill XI against Elgin Works Ladies. Charleston was promised a public toilet and visitors were banned from the Dunfermline and West Fife hospital because of a flu outbreak. The first person to be prosecuted for an offence relating to pedestrian crossings was fined five shillings. An apprentice grocer, the driver of a pedal bicycle, 'failed to allow free and uninterrupted passage to three children who were foot passengers on the crossing.'

D.C.I. opened new tea rooms in Dunfermline with four floors and an electric lift, and The Marx Brothers were at The Regal with *A Night at the Opera*. A week before *Mutiny on the Bounty* was shown in Dunfermline, actor Alec Y. Craig was interviewed about his role as 'McCoy.' Originally from Pilmuir Street, Craig had lived for many years in Los Angeles and had parts in a number of films including *The Little Minister* and *Little Lord Fauntleroy*.

As part of The Scottish Community Dramatic Association competition, The First Dunfermline Rangers Company presented a play whose title deserved a prize for originality - *Six Who Pass While the Lentils Boil*.

The Great Levante, who had 'dived off Lambeth Bridge into the Thames, handcuffed,' amazed with a series of bewildering magical mysteries.

Willie Pantzer and the greatest little troupe of Lilliputian artists, the world's only performing bullock, yodellers, acro-comedians, phantom rope trick artistes, clog dancers, Doris and her zebra - all made their way to Dunfermline, strutted their little hour upon the stage and were gone.

More illustrious visitors included the Scottish Orchestra under its conductor John, later Sir John, Barbirolli.

When the theatre opened in August after the summer break, the new manager was R.G. Walker. O'Driscoll resigned his directorship of the Opera Company in September though his financial commitment continued for another two years.

The new manager had a long connection with the theatrical profession and had spent the summer months preparing for the task ahead. He visited principal theatres and engaged artistes and companies to provide a programme of variety, plays and musical comedies, with pantomimes for the Christmas and New Year season.

For the opening week, the principal act was to be *The Ganjou Brothers and Juanita*. This quartet of adagio dancers played every top class venue in the world, and many people tried unsuccessfully to copy their act.

It featured a giant mantelpiece and a huge clock, with Juanita swinging on the pendulum. She was a trained ballerina, and the Ganjous, three Polish brothers, wearing powdered wigs and Georgian outfits, would throw her from one to the other.

In the next year, new and more familiar names appear - Tommy Morgan, with his *Clairty Capers*, Tommy Yorke, Rae Francis, Jack Beattie and Frank and Doris Droy. Her voice was said to make a pneumatic road drill sound like the purring of a contented cat.

In *Revels of 1937*, Jack Radcliffe followed a record breaking eight week season at the Empress Theatre Glasgow with a week at the Opera House. With him was Helen Norman, a niece of the great Walford Bodie.

Tommy Loman starred in *The Meltonians and* Archie McCulloch presented *Happiness in the Air* with Hughie Green's Famous BBC Gang and Broadcasting Band. More famous later as the television personality and host of *Opportunity Knocks* Hughie was a dancer and radio and film star.

Other well known radio shows that made it to the provinces were *In Town Tonight* and *Radio Pie*. In November one of the supporting acts was billed as Willie Starrs, variety's youngest accordionist, who later became the famous Will Starr.

Performers at the Opera House were often involved in the life of the town. Charlie Kemble and Tommy Lorne were among those who were invited to speak to the local Rotary Club. Kemble told them he had been born in Aberdeen, raised in Glasgow and had made most of his money from the close-fisted Fifers.

Harold Pryde

When soirees and concert entertainments flourished, many villages like Kinglassie, Buckhaven, Methil and Leslie had Saturday evening events,and as many as half a dozen of the top comedians of the day would be assembled on the platform at Thornton Station waiting for the last train to Glasgow.

Kemble recalled the concert parties arriving in Kelty and going to the secretary's house for a rehearsal, while a crowd assembled outside to listen and decide if it was worth paying to hear them again later in the evening.

He expressed his appreciation for Dunfermline audiences. Thanks to the support he had received, a two week engagement had been extended to seventeen weeks and had to be ended only because of another booking.

Tommy Lorne, like many other showbiz personalities before and since was an enthusiastic golfer and spent much of his free time on the Dunfermline Club's course.

He told how he had received his first 'attractive' fee of fifty pounds from John Henry Hare for a week's work at The Opera House. Along with other members of the company, Lorne visited the Dunfermline and West Fife Hospital to entertain the patients and promised to make a return visit next time he was in Dunfermline.

In September 1937 war, though perhaps not uppermost in people's minds, was certainly on the fringes of their consciousness. Red Cross lectures were held on chemical warfare and first aid precautions.

October saw the opening of The Carnegie Hall. A concert was followed by a week of grand opera, Handel's *Acis and Galatea* and Flotow's *Martha*, performed by The Dunfermline Amateur Opera, and then by a series of weekly chamber concerts.

Newspaper references to the Opera House performances vary, possibly depending on column space or the reporter's preferences. In November 1938, *Joy Bells* inspired the theatre reviewer to fulsome praise.

'The management of the Opera House are to be congratulated on the fare they are providing for their patrons. *Joy Bells of 1938,* this week's attraction maintains the high standard of shows which have appeared since the completion of the summer season by Charlie Kemble and his Nu-optimists.

Right from the start, Jimmy Lang and Ike Freedman put us into good humour with their witticisms. Tommy and Jimmy pull some fast wisecracks in *The Yank and the Scot* besides imparting hilarity to the sketches, while Ike Freedman's individual appearance also scored a hit.

Bessie Bendon, always popular in Dunfermline, bears her full share of the laughter making, with her wonderful character study of every complaint known to medical science. The singing of Jose Donelli, Jack Sutton and Bobby Dundas is a blend of classical and popular airs while Matt and Billie add to the success of the show with their piano-accordion duets.

Artistic dances are provided by Diana and D'Milde; the Gerrard sisters sing delightfully while the High Steppers are an efficient chorus. One of the most successful parts of the show is the Russian Revels scene in which singing and dancing is splendidly interwoven.

Next week, Harry Gordon makes his annual appearance at the Opera House.

The man frae Inversnecky needs no introducing or recommendation to Dunfermline theatregoers and it only remains to be said that he brings with him an accomplished company of entertainers.'

Harry Gordon was always a favourite. On this occasion he was aided and abetted by Jack Holden and Alex Lennox, who was 'hoofing it for his oof.' A peculiar type of 1930s slang, oof meant money so this meant he was a dancer by trade.

MATT & BILLIE.

Matt and Billie

Programmes always included troupes of dancing girls, sometimes added to by local dance academies. Reviews and variety performances, though popular, were not the only fare on offer.

The thirties saw the heyday of the repertory theatre and Dunfermline was often the starting point for national tours with plays coming directly from London theatres. Shaw, Barrie and Somerset Maugham were favourites.

The Dunfermline Amateur Elocution and Dramatic Society performed, among other offerings, *Lady Windermere's Fan* and *The Wee McGregor*.

JB Fagan presented The Irish Players with *Juno and The Paycock*. Among the many authors represented was Arnold Ridley, known to later generations as Godfrey in *Dad's Army*.

Few of his fans realised that he was a successful playwright, *Ghost Train* being perhaps his most famous production. The MacDona Players, under their famous actor manager, Charles MacDona, played six nights in Dunfermline and presented ten plays by George Bernard Shaw.

The Charles Denville Players had an enormous repertoire including *Rookery Nook, East Lynn, Daddy Long Legs* and *Charlie's Aunt*. The company's talents ranged from saucy comedies to *The Crimes of Burke and Hare,* from *Babes in the Wood* to *The Story of the Rosary.*

They had musicians as well. Between the acts of *The Barrats of Wimpole Street,* there was an overture and march, a gypsy dance and a polka.

Henry Baynton and his Shakespearian Company performed *The Merchant of Venice* with Andrew Cruickshank, later of Doctor Finlay fame as Lorenzo and A Midsummer's Night Dream with

Andrew again as Hermia's father. Harold V. Neilson presented his Shakespearian Festival Company; The O'Mara Theatre Company demonstrated the stamina needed for a touring production, with six different operas in three days, as the programme notes for 1935 show.

Mr Seymour Hicks, one of the great actor managers

Wednesday afternoon - *Faust*; Wednesday evening - *Maritana* ; Friday - *Cavalliera Rusticana* and *I Pagliacci*; Saturday afternoon - *The Bohemian Girl*; Saturday evening - *Maritana*

On their next visit in 1937 the programme read: Monday - *Carmen*; Tues - *The Barber of Seville*; Wednesday - *The Tales of Hoffman;* Thursday - *Rigoletto*

As radio became more popular, radio parades starred familiar names and radio talent contests were held with valuable prizes advertised. Charlie Kemble and his Nu-Optimist Summer Shows continued.

A producer as well as a comedian, Kemble was famous for his ability to improvise with references to members of the audience. New names were appearing - Tommy Hope, Jimmy Lang and Company, Dave Willis and Company.

Willis was one of Scotland's ace comedians and his all star company included David Dale, Jimmy McKinlay and Florence Herton.

D'Alba, a Royal Command performer who could name any article immediately in spite of being blindfolded, provided what was considered the most astounding act of the show.

In 1938, an Empire Exhibition Revue was inspired by the exhibition at Bellahouston Park in Glasgow. If people were unsatisfied by what was on offer in Dunfermline, there were rail excursions to theatres in Glasgow and Edinburgh.

A nine week spring season by The Denville Players was followed again by Charlie Kemble's Nu-Optimists. The Opera House no longer closed for an extended summer break but the pattern of entertainment offered was changing.

Summer show seasons became longer and longer, stretching from May to October, with the same cast performing for over twenty weeks at a time, with a weekly change of programme. From October to Christmas, it was non-stop variety. Bobby Telford, George West, Jack Radcliffe and Dave Willis were all welcomed as old friends.

But other things were happening. March 26th began a week designated *Rat Week* when occupiers were asked to make strenuous efforts to rid their property of rats.

Lectures and demonstrations on air raid precautions were held and pleas made for volunteers to join the ARP, first aid posts, emergency fire brigades and ambulance service. Mock air raids were organised.

By October, the Provost's Fund was raising money to aid Czechoslovakian refugees. The war, though not yet begun , was casting its shadow and by the middle of 1939, women were being asked to join the Auxiliary Territorial Service, the ATS, for general duties such as cooking, clerking and orderly work.

The Independent Labour Party held an anti - conscription rally, gas masks were issued, air raid shelters and new allotments organised. Rosyth children were evacuated and expectant mothers offered the chance to go as well.

Food and fuel control committees were set up and pigeon fanciers warned that they could not fly their birds without a licence from the police.

There was plenty, however, to distract attention from the perils ahead. Shirley Temple *in Little Miss Broadway* was showing in the Regal, one of the town's four cinemas.

The Carnegie Dunfermline Trust organised concerts and The Glasgow Orpheus Choir performed, as well as the local Choral Union. Pinders Circus came to Brucefield Showground and Samson provided incredible feats of strength at The Opera House.

The London and North Eastern Railway provided excursions to Leven, Cupar, Perth and Aberdeen. *Lilac Time* was followed by seven weeks of The Regent Players, talent spotting competitions and the ubiquitous Charlie Kemble, whose record breaking summer show ran from May 6th to December 23rd.

His two pantomimes Jack and Jill and Dick Whittington continued into the new year. There was a break, however, in this run.

Almost concurrent with the announcement of the outbreak of war on 3rd September 1939 came the news that all places of entertainment were to close immediately.

Chic Murray and Maidie

CHAPTER FIVE

BUSINESS AS USUAL

The ban on theatre opening was short lived. Within two weeks it was business as usual, with Charlie Kemble and his Nu-Optimists continuing their interrupted run.

Dunfermline's Provost expressed his satisfaction, saying that places of entertainment were necessary at such a time. Concerts were now held in aid of the Red Cross, and a Carnegie Knitting Club was formed 'to provide materials for comforts for men on service.'

On the surface, the war years saw little change in the style and tempo of the entertainment business, certainly as far as the Opera House was concerned. In January 1940, advertisements for the Opera House's pantomime, *Dick Whittington*, sit alongside more sombre notices. Air raid sirens were to be tested every month and people were asked to hand in their ration books to be sure of getting a meat supply.

Charlie Kemble and his Nu-Optimists began a nine week run, coal and coke were rationed, lectures were held on growing food in allotments and the council were offering to sell air raid shelters. The Dunfermline Light Opera company performed *Desert Song* in aid of the British Red cross and Tommy Morgan brought his *Clairty Capers*.

Born in Bridgeton, Glasgow, Morgan already had twenty years experience in variety. Much of his humour came from tenement life. With Tommy Yorke, he enjoyed a record-breaking six-month seasons for many years at the Pavilion, Glasgow and had a record nineteen successive summer shows there.

Morgan appeared in pantomime and his own shows, and encouraged many promising young entertainers including Larry Marshall, Jimmy Neil, Anne Fields, Roy Castle and Ruby Murray. One of his most famous characters was the G I Bride, 'Big Beanie McBride, the Pride of the Clyde'.

Beanie was the typical Glasgow woman, overdressed and doing all the wrong things. Tommy began the fashion of reading out dedications to people in the audience, for anniversaries, birthdays and so on. His catch phrase 'Clairty, Clairty,' derived from the phrase, 'I declare to goodness.'

During the forties The Opera House almost exclusively hosted light entertainment shows. In early 1940 these included *Spring Revels, Laughter Barrage, Scotch Breezes, and Suicide Sal and her Gang*.

Sal was Doris Droy Her husband Frank, who ran an act called The De Roy sisters and Frank, decided to form his own concert party and hired a hall in Macduff.

Their first week was a disaster and they didn't have enough money to cover the hire of the hall. The Great Doctor Walford Bodie paid the bill and offered them a part in his show. They travelled in the van with the equipment, helped put up the scenery, sold programmes, and took tickets at the door.

Doris sang songs and also played the part of a nurse during Bodie's electrical treatments. Her sister came on stage to be hypnotised by him.

When the show had a two week break they returned to Glasgow, the sister announced she was getting married and the act became Frank and Doris Droy. Together they wrote and starred in pantomime at the Queen's Theatre, Glasgow Cross before going on to star in shows like *Nae Hairm Done.*

Harry Gordon brought his *Snecky Parade* which featured the Tiller Girls, a troupe of dancers which would eventually go on to feature in the popular television show *Sunday Night At The London Palladium.*

Charlie Kemble returned, this time with his Nu-Optimist Summer show which boasted a complete change of programme every week, despite having the same performers. No small feat, considering the summer show was to continue till the end of October.

This pattern was to be repeated over the next few years. Winter shows included Christmas and New Year pantomimes and January saw Burns weeks or Scotch nights. Lack of manpower did not seem to affect the industry which was probably dependent on older performers and those ineligible for active service.

By June 1940, coal, coke and petrol were rationed, lectures were given on growing food in allotments and the council were selling air raid shelters.

Patersons of East Port were telling their customers that radio was no longer a luxury but a necessity. For under ten pounds you could have up to the minute news and entertainment at your fingertips.

One effect of radio was the introduction of radio personalities. George Elrick, advertised as 'the smiling voice of radio', appeared in The Kinema Ballroom and The Ice Rink as well as the Opera House.

Carroll Levis and his BBC discoveries appeared in March 1941 and Jack Radcliffe and Company presented *S'up Wi You* in May.

Bert Denver

Brought up in Bellshill, Radcliffe began acting in Kinderspiels and sang with the Baptist Male Voice Choir. After leaving school he tried several jobs, including mining and was on maintenance work at a Lanarkshire pit when the general strike of 1926 began.

He joined a concert party and on one occasion is said to have hired an ice cream van to get to a show, was late getting back to work and got sacked. Jack went on to work with almost every comic in Scotland and billed himself as 'Scotland's Greatest Comedian.'

He was invited to appear at a Royal Command performance, an unusual honour for a Scots comedian, and teamed up with Jimmy Logan in the *Half Past Eight* revues. He took to wearing white tie and tails and was known as 'the Scottish William Powell'.

In October Gloria Gaye and Her All Ladies Swing Band followed the Nu-Optimist Summer Show, and *Thumbs Up* offered 'thought readers, fan dancers, Tarzan the man monkey, accordionists, girls and novelties.'

The Opera House had to compete against an ever growing number of attractions. As well as four cinemas, Dunfermline boasted concerts, classes at The Music Institute, and an ice rink, used both for skating and dancing.

There were dances in the co-operative halls, Red Cross dances, tea dances, a Cafe Chantant and the Carnegie knitting club. For families, there were also visits from Bertha Waddell's Children's Theatre.

With the arrival of Polish soldiers, came concerts by the Polish Army Choir. Throughout the war years, a series of lectures were given by the Israeli World Federation for Scotland.

Not even Sundays were exempt. A series of performances, concerts, variety shows and pantomimes, *Sunday night at 7,* were begun in December 1941, and later changed to *Sunday Night at 6.* Held on behalf of the Lord Provost's Fund they raised money for the Russian Red Cross and various other charities.

People were probably glad to escape from the world of increasing shortages. Cheese and jam were rationed, and so was clothing. Gardeners were told to grow vegetables instead of flowers, people encouraged to keep bees so honey could be used as a substitute for sugar and beekeepers were given sugar rations for their hives.

People were even being exhorted to give up their books for salvage. Old age pensioners who had children under five in their care could apply for free milk, while expectant and nursing mother could buy a pint for two pence.

Compulsory immunisation for children against diphtheria was introduced and pensioners and the poor were given indoor air raid shelters. The Ministry of Food allowed restaurants to open two hours a day and a three course meal could be had for one shilling and one penny. Dining cars on trains were withdrawn.

People were asked to help buy a destroyer HMS Malcolm, and there was a public notice about the increasing prevalence of venereal diseases and an outbreak of smallpox in Fife.

Special shows were put on. In December 1943 the Winter Show produced a tribute to the 51st Division.

Earlier that year, George Cunningham had joined the Opera House as producer in succession to Charles L. West who resigned because of ill health. An Edinburgh man, Cunningham made the summer and winter shows that year the most successful in its history.

In twenty weeks there were sixty complete changes of programme including a spectacular production *The Gathering of the Clans* in which Cunningham 'played to perfection a Perthshire shepherd,' and *Charlie's Farewell to Scotland,* which met with tremendous success. Cunningham was an able compere, splendid vocalist and gifted elocutionist. His first job was to produce the Burns Anniversary Show. His wife was an accompanist and the couple were well known in Dunfermline, having appeared at The Services Theatre in Carnegie Hall.

The Winter Show, *Shamrock & Heather* starred Tommy Hope and Jimmy Lang, Bobby Wotherspoon, Billy Bowers, Joan Morton, George Cunningham, Dean, Dixon and Day; Patricia Ford, Eight Dryburgh Girls, Muriel Cronshaw and Jackson Manley.

In the same year, Robert Wilson, billed as *The Voice of Scotland* made his first appearance in The Opera House, and among the lesser acts appearing was one Beryl Reid, later to achieve fame as a film and television actress.

Will Fyffe came, 'direct from the front line in Italy,' and was supported by Jack Beattie and Denis Gordon. Bessie Audley, a BBC pianist in 1944 was said to be 'just repatriated from a German prison camp.'

On the same bill was the radio recording star, Master Joe Peterson. During the 1930s, Joe rose to fame as a boy soprano with an angelic voice, filled theatres and sold thousands of records during his career. Reviewers gushed over his performances and Joe was a crowd puller in every theatre he appeared in. One description of his stage appearances said that there would be a hush in the theatre when he was about to take the stage. The band would strike up his signature tune *Choirboy,* and the curtains would open to reveal his tiny figure, dressed in black jacket and trousers, white shirt and bow tie.

By all accounts he had an extraordinary voice but what was more extraordinary was that in a career lasting more than nine years, he continued to sing soprano long after his voice should have broken. What the crowds who flocked to hear the boy wonder didn't know was a 'secret' known to the Music Hall fraternity but carefully hidden from the theatre going, record buying public. Little Joe was in fact Mary Lethbridge from Helensburgh, who was married and had a daughter.

Born Mary O'Rourke, she went to London when still in her teens, and married a Londoner, George Lethbridge. In Islington, she met an uncle, Ted Stebbings, whose career as a singer ended when his voice broke and he persuaded her to pose as a boy. She was only five foot tall and made a convincing boy.

Audiences were completely fooled and every new record was greeted with universal acclaim. Why no-one ever questioned the possibility of a teenage boy with an unbroken soprano voice continuing to perform for nine years is peculiar.

Mary found it difficult to cope with her fame and no doubt with the strain of maintaining her double life. She began to drink, and deserted by her husband, ended up in Glasgow, singing in Bingo halls. Mary died in 1963 aged fifty three, and was buried as a pauper in an unmarked grave, her fame forgotten.

In 1998, a Newcastle journalist uncovered the story of her double life and compiled a CD of her recordings. Lismor, the Glasgow based record company, then paid for a gravestone for Mary's grave in Dalbeath cemetery in Maryhill. The inscription reads: 'Mary Lethbridge, known to her millions of fans as Master Joe Peterson.'

Master Jo Petersen

Dave Willis appeared, 'fresh from his tour with the forces' and the programme for November 11th included Kardroma, described as the patriotic illusionist.

Willis made a number of return visits, as an individual performer or as part of The Troon Entertainers. Shows with titles like *Salute to The Navy,* and *The Air Force on Parade* were popular.

In April 1945 a show called *Fig Leaves and Apple Sauce* was billed as a new style, up to date road show. Hosted by Pierre Cordell, 'the Famous Canadian Trickster,' with his electrified crazy gang, it offered patrons an electric chair from Sing Sing, and 'married by electricity'. Also on view were Gordon Norvals Eight Pin Up Cuties.

Two weeks later *Just For Fun*, said to be another entirely new road revue featured George West, a Glasgow comedian who began his stage career with Tommy Lorne at amateur Saturday nights in The Grand Theatre in Cowcaddens.

Punters who didn't like them threw potatoes or bits of clay pipe, so they soon learned to cope with rejection. He spent some time clog dancing before realising that comedy was a lot less work.

A prize for a comic song performance brought him his first engagement and he became a successful imitator. He was a great clown, with elaborate make-up and clothes, and a part in a pantomime at The Princess's Theatre led to a sixteen year residence as comedian there.

His last appearance was in a pantomime which ran for a record twenty one weeks, just before the theatre was leased to The Glasgow Citizen's Theatre. That was followed by his two week visit to Dunfermline.

On May 5th, 1945, notice of the 'Celebration of the Termination of Organised Hostilities in Europe' was advertised. So, too, was the formal 'adoption' of Trondheim by Dunfermline and District Youth Organisations. The following week, householders were told they could demolish their air raid shelters at their own expense.

In The Opera House, the summer show with George Burton and Jim Logan continued with no apparent nod to outside events.

On September 8th, after a break of many years, repertory theatre returned with Frank H Fortescue's Famous Players and *Rebecca*. Over the next three months they presented a programme of ten plays including *Jane Eyre, Wuthering Heights, The Corn is Green, Ten Little Niggers* and *The Patsy*.

Then it was back to The Winter Show with Bobby Telford. Unlike the early days of the Opera House when dozens of touring repertory companies appeared week after week, programmes now consisted mainly of summer and winter shows, whose titles changed but the cast remained the same. They were hosted by a 'star' comedian - Pete Martin, Jimmy Lang, Tommy Hope, George West, Aly Wilson, Tommy Loman and Billy Denison - to name but a few.

The space between summer and winter shows was filled by companies like Fortescue's Repertory Players, Harold G. Roberts Gaiety Players, and from 1947, The Charles Denville Players, all performing a different play each week - from *Rebecca, Arsenic and Old Lace and The Winslow Boy* to *The Dominant Sex* - billed as suitable for adults only.

L-R- Arthur Spink, Dennis Clancy, Rob Coburn, Joss Esplin, Alec Finlay, Will Starr

Occasional one or two week shows filled the gaps: The Five Smith Brothers, or Mr and Mrs Smith's Five Little Boys; The Ralph Reader Gang Show and odd characters like Cire - The Emperor of Mystery; Jagana, The Man with a Miracle Mind and St Clair, the famous hypnotist.

In January 1949, the winter show had to compete with Dunfermline's own film star. Showing in The Palace Kinema for 'positively six days only' was Moira Shearer in *The Red Shoes.*

Ballet was becoming important as was dancing of all kinds, with dancing schools proliferating. There were Palais de Dances in Cowdenbeath, Rosyth, Burntisland and Aberdour as well as various clubs and halls in Dunfermline.

With five cinemas and an ice rink, which also had dancing twice a week, there was no shortage of entertainment.

For those of a political bent, there were meetings in support of The Scottish Covenant, with speakers including Nigel Tranter, Abe Moffatt and Willie Gallacher, who was standing as electoral candidate for West Fife.

There were morning meetings for back shift miners with slogans like 'better support the best man' and 'come and hear this grand speaker' and special afternoon meetings for ladies who could not be expected to cope with the hurly burly of male hustings.

Dunfermline Dramatic Society presented *Hedda Gabler*, and audiences were 'amazed, amused and convinced by Cliff Leslie, the brilliant exponent of hypnotism.'

One of the cast of *Rosie O'Grady* in March 1950 was Jack Milroy who made several appearances in Dunfermline. Born in Glasgow, Milroy made his name in the summer seasons at the Tivoli, Aberdeen, as a solo comic in *Whirl of Laughter* from 1950 to 1952. That year he married Mary Lee who sang with Roy Fox and the Moxon Dance Band during the thirties.

In 1953, they starred in a twenty-two week Tivoli *Whirl* season and this success began a stage partnership lasting over thirty years.

Later they starred in *King's High*, a series of summer revues at the Glasgow King's in which Jack revived his role as Francie to Rikki Fulton's Josie.

The characters Francie and Josie, Glasgow wide boys of the fifties, as played by Milroy and Fulton, made their first appearance in 1960 and their double act became one of the most celebrated of the Scottish Variety stage.

Rikki Fulton also hailed from Glasgow and made his debut as an amateur actor at the Lyric theatre in Sauchiehall Street, which led to a four year BBC contract in the late forties. Pantomime and scriptwriting gave him a taste for comedy, and a ten year career with the Howard & Wyndham Company.

Francie and Josie made both Fulton and Jack Milroy household names after it moved from stage to television in the early sixties.

Subsequently Fulton's own BBC Scotland television series, *Scotch and* Wry, in which he appeared in many character roles including the famous Reverend I. M. jolly, proved perennially popular. Rikki Fulton was thought by many to be the finest Scots comedian of his generation.

A visit from the Glasgow Unity Theatre in May 1950 starred Roddy McMillan, Bill Anderson,

Shenah Dalgleish and Andrew Keir. In July, Arthur Lax, the musical director and his Opera House Orchestra performed in Pittencrieff Park; the fleet was in at Rosyth with cruisers, aircraft carriers and large modern destroyers. Greer Garson and Errol Flynn were in *The Forsyte Saga* at the Alhambra.

Two weeks after a new school at Ballingry was built, at a cost of £182,000, it was flooded when a culvert was blocked. The Lochty Burn filled the boiler room which was eighteen feet below ground level and classrooms were fourteen inches deep in water. Areas in Dunfermline in Rosyth were also affected as 'fountains of water issued from gulleys and manholes in the road.'

In an article called 'Go Ahead And Yell', a reader has a complaint with a modern ring to it.

'Now the railways are nationalised - if your train is consistently ten minutes late and your boss doesn't believe this is possible of a nationalised railway, you can go on complaining. But where do you complaints go?'

There were *Ban The Bomb* meetings and demands for newspaper to be salvaged. Frank H. Fortescue brought his repertory company for a twelve week run, The Ballet Rambert was in The Carnegie Hall and new ultra-violet lighting was introduced.

Opera House Summer Show visitors included Ian Richardson who became a character actor and television star with programmes like *The Procurator Fiscal*; Robert Wilson, whose shows at The Carnegie Hall were sold out; and Duncan Macrae in *Bachelors Bold* fresh from his success at the Edinburgh Festival.

The stage manager for that show was Russell Hunter and even the cigarettes and nylons were given a mention in the credits

One of the popular shows was *The McFlannels Hogmanay*, based on the very successful Scottish radio series.

As well as visiting repertory companies, there were a number of local groups, among them The Rosyth Dockyard Players, Perth Theatre Company, The Craig Players, and The Civil Service Society Players. A plethora of music societies also performed regularly.

Many theatre companies made use of local talent, dancers and comics, and in the fifties, Jimmy Logan ran a series of 'discoveries' to find this talent. Born in 1928, the son of the famous music-hall double act, Jack Short and May Dalziel, Jimmy learned to play the accordion and from the age of six appeared in his parents' touring summer shows in Ireland.

He did a cowboy act at ten and assisted backstage and front of house, selling chocolates and ice cream. During a show at the Glasgow Metropole, a film producer was looking for a young Glasgow actor to play in a shipyard drama. As a result, Jimmy appeared in *Floodtide* and then in a BBC comedy series, and became a household name.

For his later solo comedy career he took the name Logan from his Aunt Ella, a Broadway star. Once he had made his name, the 'Logan Family' company under Ma and Pa Logan staged many long seasons at the Metropole Theatre, Glasgow. He introduced several new and established entertainers and the Loganbelle dancers.

Jimmy Logan appeared in films and in the successful radio series, *It's All Yours,* before joining

Howard and Wyndham for pantomime and *Five Past Eight* shows. Established as a top entertainer by 1964, he moved into theatre management, at one time seriously considering buying the Opera House.

He did buy the Empress Theatre, Glasgow and re-named it The New Metropole. With the days of variety numbered, Jimmy Logan presented a series of musicals, and light comedies before closing the theatre in 1970.

Jimmy Logan

Subsequently he produced and starred in successful farces during the summer months, appeared as Sir Harry Lauder in a one-man show at the Edinburgh Festival and toured Scotland as Archie Rice in John Osborne's *The Entertainer.*

In Dunfermline, where he had made his debut in 1945, Logan held auditions and about twenty five acts were judged, the best then appearing at the Opera House. New dancers, singers and musicians were supported by a variety company consisting of Hal Mack and his Dancing Demons whose speciality was tip top tap, the Fraser Hayes Quartet of radio fame, and Billy Rusk, comedian.

Snippets of history continue to intrude. In September 1952, the Boys Brigade presented a fanfare in support of the Lynmouth disaster, when almost a whole village in the south of England was wiped out by exceptionally high tides.

The Johnny Victory show began a short season. Johnny was a comedian and crooner, one of Carrol Levis's discoveries, who quickly became popular. He co-starred with Robert Wilson in a fourteen week show at the Tivoli, Aberdeen, and was resident comedian there till 1963, achieving a record of eighty one weekly appearances.

One of his stock characters was 'Pierre, ze great lovaire', another a statue of McGonagall in conversation with Robert Burns. Assisting Johnny at the Opera House was his new feed Hector Nicol, who after acting as a straight man for many years, became famous as a clubland comic with risque jokes, bawdy humour and an inexhaustible flow of one liners.

Others on the bill were Betty Nolan, comedienne; Matt Soutar, accordionist; Desmond Carrol and Jean Davis, dancers; Anthony Tuppen and Lillian Jeans, vocalists; the McDonald sisters, dancers and vocalists; Stan Mars and Irene Hall, comedy vocalists; and the dance troupe.

In 1953, Johnny Beattie appeared in Dunfermline for the first time in *Tommy Comes To Town*, three-D films were introduced and a coronation service of thanksgiving was held in theAbbey.

Back from Korea where they were entertaining the troops, says one advert, are Alex Munro and Tommy Wills, famous radio, revue and pantomime comedians and knockabouts.

A good example of changing fashions is the inclusion in the line up of Dykes (Bouncer) Andrews, exponent of the trampoline art.

Renee Houston and Donald Stewart brought a short lived return of Variety and novelty acts, their show including an Electronic Organist, Palette's Poodles, Rondart, the darts blower and Peter Sinclair, 'The Cock of the North'. Sinclair played Jimmy Clitheroe's grandfather in the long running radio show.

Many novelty acts like these have disappeared without trace. Who today has heard of Frederick Ferrar, one time star of the Charlie Chester Show, or Herschel Henlere, the King of Jizz, star pianist of the Moss Empire theatres?

On September 12th, 1953, the Opera House celebrated its fiftieth anniversary with a cast of relatively unknown stars - Archie Lewis, Jackie Wilson, Dinkie Maurice, Stefano, Foster and Clark, Christine Granville, Douglas Harris, Reid Twins, Tiki and Del.

The Dunfermline Press recalled the high points of the theatre's fifty years, starting with the opening performance when the Dunfermline Amateur Dramatic Society first occupied its stage with *A Friend in Need* and *Cramond Brig.*.

'This building, which has undergone many changes during its half century, today occupies an important place in providing entertainment not only in Dunfermline but in the whole of Fife.

Jimmy Reid and Tommy Loman

It is the only permanently established theatre in the area. A number of alterations have been made, including the removal of the side galleries which brought the capacity down to about half of its original thirteen hundred.

While variety undoubtedly appears to appeal to its present day patrons there will be many who remember the splendid performances of light opera and musical comedies of pre war years. Under Henry Hare, outstanding musical comedies were staged and performances of Shaw's plays drew large audiences.

It is to be regretted that repertory seasons, presented from time to time have found only limited support because they offered the public an excellent introduction to some of the best known dramatic works. Theatre declined with the advent of film and talkies were substituted for flesh and blood performances.

The present manager is Robert G. Walker who came to Dunfermline in 1936. From Glasgow, he has a circus background, he was involved in entertainment from the age of five and his first performance was in *Ali Baba and the Forty Thieves* at the Theatre Royal.

He joined the Howard and Wyndham company in the old Royalty Theatre in Sauchiehall Street. He had a thorough grounding in stage properties and scenery making, then in the business side of management. At various times he was transferred to the Kings and Royal Theatres.

In 1910 he joined the R.C. Buchanan circuit which combined silent films and theatre business. About 1919 he went to the King's, Dundee when it was still a music hall and was acting manager for four years, then general and booking manager for six and a half years. When the King's was sold he joined the Bostock circuit and had charge of halls in Hamilton, Paisley and Blantyre and for a time managed Glasgow's second largest cinema, The Astoria.

Later he went touring and managed comedian Tommy Morgan for a spell. After being in Dunfermline for two months, he went for seven months to take charge of The Palace Theatre in Dundee, before returning to The Opera House.'

The star of the anniversary concert was Archie Lewis, a singer with Geraldo's radio and television band, and a supporting cast of unknowns. Variety over the next weeks was provided by The Logan family, Lex Mclean and His Happy Gang and Clarke and Murray, whose cast included Larry Marshall.

Winter shows gave way to pantomime and new comedians came and went. Jack Radcliffe made a return visit, with Helen Norman. In February 1954, the press reported that 'the new Billy Stutt show which opened on Monday should be popular - plenty of fun, good singing, bright music andattractive dancing. Billy Stutt is a first class Irish comedian and he has a grand collaborator in Johnnie Beattie. Eileen Clare, Irish comedienne is another sparkling personality with a shrewd knowledge of how to get laughs from audiences.

Alberto plays the accordion; Lloyd Day, TV and cabaret star sings to his own piano accompaniment; Sylvia Norman, soprano; Richard Hardie, BBC baritone; Dean, Dixon and Day whose navy ways, while unorthodox, are most enjoyable as they cavort and dance; and The Moxon Dance Troupe.'

Billy Stutt gave way in March to a new repertory theatre company, referred to as The Rex Deering Repertory Company or The Rex Deering Crown Players.

As well as light comedies, they tackled more demanding roles, some advertised as suitable for adults only. *Reefer Girl* was the story of a drug addict, while *Vice on the Street* was given an X rating. The Deering Players introduced two names well known in Dunfermline, Denise Coffey and Freda Drysdale, of whom, more later.

After a twenty week season, repertory was replaced by variety again, this time a three week run of *Mixed Grill*, a song, dance and comedy show provided by a local amateur concert party. The Press reported that Manager Robert Walker had got together a company which he felt sure would appeal to a wide variety of tastes.

The comedy was in the capable hands of Jack Dougary from Lochgelly, and also in the line up was Francis Barr from Izatt Avenue who had won the Glen talent competition with 'his grand whistling performance.'

More variety followed. *Bonnie Scotch Lassie o Mine,* with an all-tartan, all musical, all laughter finale, featured The Alexander Brothers.

Kenneth McKellar made a flying visit with *Flying High* and a star variety show presented Master Jo Peterson and, very far down the bill, Andy Stewart, the new BBC comic. *Marching Thro The Heather* presented Alan Gordon, known as the Scottish Caruso. Johnny Victory and Hector Nicol made a return visit.

Johnny Beattie also returned, further up the bill this time, and Aly Wilson began a series of *Comedy Capers.* Jack Dougary's *Mixed Grill* made a welcome reappearance with Ronnie Parnell and the added attraction of Tommy Daniels, the singing cowboy.

In January 1955, another new repertory company appeared, The Easdale Theatre Company from Darlington with *Two Dozen Red Roses*, by Kenneth Horne.

A long time star of radio, Horne was famous for his programme *Round The Horn,* written by Barry Took and co-starring Kenneth Williams, Hugh Paddick and Betty Marsden. Easdale's four week season saw the last drama performances in The Opera House.

Daniel Connell presented The Canmore Youth Club Discoveries, twenty three young people who hoped to be the stars of tomorrow. On March 12th, the Opera House management regretted that because they could not find a suitable attraction for the entire week, there would be three performances only of a grand variety show, one on Friday and two on Saturday.

On the 19th, George Cormack and Irene Sharp headed a cast which included Master Joe Peterson, the Singing Choirboy, and Andy Stewart, still billed as a comedian, .

The last ever show in the Opera House took place on March 26th, 1955. It has a bottom of the barrel feel about it. Starring were Margaret Ann-Brown, Larry Marshall, Uncle Willie Lindsay, Tony Kenny - billed as Scotland's wee comic, and George Simpson, The Singing Postie.

In May, the death was announced of Arthur Stanley Lax, who had been musical director since September 1941.

He had served in the first world war, spent some time in Burma and was at one time Musical Director to Governor General of Burma.

Lax played the piano and cinema organ, used to play in Glasgow picture houses, was associated with several cinema orchestras in Scotland. For a time, he had his own orchestra on one of the Clyde pleasure steamers.

He had a collection of over ten thousand pieces of music, and wrote and arranged music for variety artistes and for the Boy Scout Gang Shows. He toured Scotland with variety shows and was at one time manager of Walford Bodie.

But it was not just the musical director that died. The rise of television had sounded the death knell for variety and theatre audiences diminished rapidly, not just in Dunfermline, but everywhere in the country. On April 2nd, the press announced that The Opera House was closed temporarily. It was never to reopen.

~ Opera House ~

Dunfermline

Manager ... ... Mr. RG Walker

Tonight (Saturday) 26th March 1955

6.30 Twice Nightly 8.30

Grand Variety Show

Margaret Ann - Brown

Wullie Lindsay

Trudi Gaye

George Simpson

Tommy Kenny

St. Dennis Sisters

Jean Elliott

Larry Marshall

Book Early

Stalls 3/6   Circle 3/-   Pit 1/9   Gallery 1/-

The end of the road -
the playbill for the last performance

Athur Lax with some of the stars of the Opera House – including Carr and Vonnie; Chris Johnston.
Binnie Stephen, Agnes McDermott, Archie Roy, Sheila Whitely, Bernard Ross, Jimmy Vincent,
Betty Morton, Gladys Garside, Renee Horrox and Bobby Telford

CHAPTER SIX
SAVE THE OPERA HOUSE CAMPAIGNS

The Opera House closed in 1955 and liquidation proceedings began in August the following year.

The main problem for the liquidators was the sale of the property, which was made difficult by the depressed conditions in the theatre world, particularly in provincial areas. Only one offer was made but was withdrawn because financial backing could not be guaranteed.

The theatre lay empty and deserted till an offer from James Bell and Son to purchase the property for £2250.00 was accepted in 1958. Bell then presented the planning committee with an application to change the use of the building, and it became an upholsterer and cabinetmakers works with a showroom and shop front.

The news of the proposed change of use sparked off the 'Save The Opera House Appeal', spearheaded by Denise Coffey, an actress who had made her debut in the theatre as one of The Rex Deering Crown Players.

She suggested in a letter to The Parks and Entertainments Committee that the building be converted into a Civic Theatre and centre for local clubs, but they recommended that no action be taken.

A lengthy correspondence in the local newspapers followed. Letters included one from R.G. Walker, who had been the theatre's last manager, and who said that the closure had been a great loss to the theatrical and variety minded people not just of Dunfermline and District but from Kirkcaldy and Alloa as well, and drew attention to the fact that the BBC had become interested. They were to broadcast a programme about the Opera House in their Scottish Home Service programme *'Scope'* on 12th March.

In the same edition, The *'Observer'* column noted Miss Coffey was 'a young woman with a purpose. She is a talented actress, at present working with the BBC in Edinburgh. Perhaps she has left her fight to save Dunfermline's only theatre a little late but she is now putting all her energy into seeking practical support for her efforts.'

One letter summed up the feelings of many people. 'It is indeed a sorry state of affairs when a town the size and importance of Dunfermline finds itself unable and unwilling to make an effort to save this little theatre the ignominy of being turned into a shopping centre.'

Others were just as succinct. 'It would be far better to try and ease the unemployment situation instead of trying to save a theatre which in its declining years, was something of a white elephant. Sentimentality has no place in matters such as this.'

But there were sentimentalists, as described in this article by J. B. published in April 1958. 'There must be many older folk in Dunfermline and District who, like myself, regard with regret the closing of The Dunfermline Opera House.

Front and rear views of Opera House building

The publicity to which the Reform Street Theatre has been subjected in recent weeks has doubtless revived pleasant memories among citizens who, in the course of the last fifty odd years, bestowed their patronage upon the theatre which was the enterprise of the brothers Anderson, a local firm of builders.

If memory serves me right, the early years of its history were not notably successful, chiefly because the standard of equipment and facilities for artistes did not meet the requirements of leading touring theatrical companies...

Without attempting to place them in order of appearance on the stage of the Opera House during the half century of its career, I recall with pleasure the performances by the George Edwards touring companies of the famous musical comedies which thrilled theatre patrons in the early part of the century. Who does not recall with pleasure such shows as *The Merry Widow, Floradora, The Dairymaids, The Arcadians, A Country Girl* and *The Belle of New York.*

Among opera companies, I recall the O'Mara and Moody-Manners combinations, who staged a first class selection of popular operas. There were visiting companies in which the late John Clyde and Durward Lely and other well-known actors played leading roles while still at the height of their fame.

Occasional repertory seasons were always welcomed by patrons, the Charles Denville and The Fortescue Players I have particularly in mind, who were privileged to witness a standard of performance which often equalled that of the more celebrated London companies which visited Edinburgh and Glasgow.

The Christmas and New Year pantomimes were always highlights in the entertainment fare of the folk of Dunfermline and surrounding districts. Nor must I forget the summer and winter season variety shows which attracted many visitors to the town.

Famous theatrical and music hall artistes were frequent visitors to the Opera House. Among them I have pleasant recollections of Sir Harry Lauder, Harry Gordon, Tommy Lorne, Will Fyffe, Charlie Kemble, Tommy Morgan, Florrie Forde, and more recently, Dave Willis, Jack Radcliffe, Jimmy Logan, Tommy Hope, Jimmy Lang, Aly Wilson and Robert Wilson.

Might I add my sincere regret that in her 'Save The Opera House' campaign, Miss Denise Coffey met with such a disappointing response.'

But despite sentimental appeals, and Miss Coffey's strenuous efforts, the planning committee's recommendation was that James Bell's application be granted, on condition that the premises be used solely for light industrial purposes. The use of the building was to be reviewed at the end of ten years.

On April 12th the Dunfermline Press reported 'The Save the Opera House campaign has failed and instead of being converted into a civic theatre and club centre the fifty five year old theatre will become a furniture factory.'

Miss Coffey had written a letter to the Town Planning Committee suggesting deferment of consideration for a month the application to turn it into an into an upholsterer and cabinetmakers works, so plans for a civic theatre could be set up, but her suggestion was turned down.

The committee granted the application of James Bell & Sons to change the use of the building and for the next twenty years the wonderful fabric of the Opera House was hidden under the shell which housed the factory.

In 1981, the spotlight once again shone on Dunfermline Opera House for plans were going ahead to ring down the final curtain on the theatre. The building was seen to stand in the way of a major improvement, the multi-million pound development of the town centre.

Dunfermline, apparently, desperately needed a new shopping centre and bus station, and the site chosen included space taken up by part of the Opera House.

Crudens, the developers eventually chosen to carry out the planned improvements, requested permission to demolish the Opera House, which had been granted List B status and therefore could not be destroyed without permission.

The District Council's Planning Committee were in favour of demolition but as soon as the news became public, there was an outcry. Part of the town's history since 1903, the theatre had for over forty years, played host to the biggest and brightest stars of stage and radio.

For most of its history, however, it had been beset with financial difficulties and the coming of television marked a steep decline in live entertainment, not just in Dunfermline but all over the country.

Alterations had been made to accommodate its new use as a workshop but the auditorium remained basically unchanged, and when the question of the future of the Opera House was raised again in 1981, several preservation societies expressed an interest.

Representations and objections came from the Scottish Georgian Society, The Theatres Trust, the Scottish Arts Council and Saltire Society on behalf of the Advisory Council for the Arts In Scotland., A request was made for the theatre to be mothballed till the financial climate was more favourable to the possibility of restoration.

The Scottish Georgian Society objected to the shopping centre development project as a whole. The demolition of The Opera House would result in the loss of historic buildings with no guarantee that the proposed shopping complex would go ahead. If the new commercial centre did proceed, the theatre could be incorporated into it and would act as a magnet in the evenings encouraging extended use.

Dunfermline, they said, lacked a facility for public theatre productions and financial help could come from the Historic Buildings Council of Scotland. Other groups regretted the decision to demolish the theatre at a time when there was an upsurge of interest in the arts in Scotland.

In his representation, Harry McCann, Deputy Director of The Scottish Arts Council said, ' I know this is a difficult time to be looking for finance from local authorities, private sector and, for that matter, the Arts Council but is it possible to mothball the building for a period and bring together members of the community who would be prepared to work towards raising funds for repairing and refurbishing the theatre.

We have no doubt that this theatre, suitably refurbished would prove to be a tremendous asset to Dunfermline and the catchment area and would hope therefore, that your authority would take steps to see that it is not demolished.'

If saved, the Opera House would be able to play host to Britain's largest and most famous orchestras, ballet and theatre companies. Top touring companies such as Scottish Ballet and Scottish Theatre had indicated that they would consider hiring the modernised Opera House for their productions.

Because it was a listed building, demolition could only take place with the consent of the Secretary of State for Scotland who could, if he wished, call in the application and hold a public local inquiry. In September 1981, the Scottish Arts Council commissioned a report into the possible future of the Opera House from Theatre Projects Consultants.

Based in London, the firm had a Scottish Director, Iain Mackintosh, who wrote the report in collaboration with Professor James Dunbar-Nasmith, a partner of the Edinburgh architects Law and Dunbar-Nasmith.

Mackintosh was well aware of the theatre's existence, having been responsible for the *Curtains!!!* project. Begun in 1976 as a protest at the failure of the authorities to halt the erosion of the theatrical gems scattered throughout the country, the project was sparked off by the announcement by the government of a reduction of almost one third in the Housing The Arts allocation.

After a letter to The Times, stressing the fact that what little was left of the dwindling stock of theatres, was under threat, a number of interested parties came together, and almost at once discovered that no inventory of theatres existed. Although a number of surveys had been begun, none was ever completed or published.

Part of a ceiling panel

An Act of Parliament in 1976 had produced a Theatres Trust, with no idea of what buildings there were to entrust, and no money earmarked for conservation purposes. Its main function was to advise local authorities on proposals for demolition or change of use and in any case, its remit didn't extend to Scotland. Theatres have no special form of protection, and measures urged by the Theatres Advisory Council and other bodies have never reached the statute books.

One of the partners in the *Curtains!!!* Project was Christopher Brereton, who visited Dunfermline in 1981. His report on the Opera House says that 'although the exterior is not exciting, a plain two storey frontage to Reform Street, flanked by little pavilions, the auditorium is very successful. It is of particular interest in that it is still wholly a theatre, showing very little sign of the influence of contemporary cinema building.'

Jackson's 1900 auditorium had two balconies supported on iron columns, stage boxes and a domed ceiling. In his reconstruction, Swanston replaced these with cantilevered balconies; changed the form of the ceiling, boxes and proscenium arch and included decorative plasterwork in a Louis XV style. Brereton described the Opera House as 'one of the most attractive medium sized theatres in Scotland.'

It was, he said, 'restorable and just about the right size for the population of the town.' However, it was in danger of being lost to an 'old-fashioned 1960s style comprehensive development.' He was convinced of the importance of little theatres to the cultural life of towns.

The Scottish Arts Council report raised this question with a number of others, the first of these being how important and rare was the Dunfermline Opera House?

The answer was that though it was constructed of brick and stone and had made use of some of the existing tenement walls for the enclosing walls, the interior, both architecturally and acoustically, was rare enough to be preserved.

Built by Roy Jackson, the Architect and Theatrical Manager of Perth Theatre, it resembled the Perth building in general concept and layout. Extensive alterations were carried out, however, in 1921 when a block was built to the west containing a projection room, a circle lounge and escape stair. The inside of the auditorium was gutted, the gallery re-raked and extended and the circle was re-planned and the pillars supporting the gallery removed in order to improve the sight-lines.

The interior was refurbished with considerable skill by the architect, Mr J. W. Swanston who, together with Davidson, had been responsible some sixteen years earlier for the extremely distinguished Kings Theatre, Edinburgh. It was this interior which survived and provided such an intimate atmosphere with excellent sight-lines and acoustics.

The building was in a poor condition. Since it closed in 1955 it had been used as a furniture warehouse and workshop and, during that time, little or no maintenance had been carried out on the fabric of the building.

Alterations had been made to the interior to facilitate its new use. The roof was no longer watertight and there were areas of dry rot and wood worm infestation. Surveyors had not been able to gain access to the building in order to carry out a structural survey, but the main structural walls were sound and there was little doubt that the interior could be restored, given adequate funds.

For the theatre to be brought fully up to modern standards, a tremendous amount of work would be required The stage, which had a fly-

Box door and some of the beautiful mirror mouldings

tower, was small, the front-of-house accommodation inadequate, and the escape stairs would require modification to comply with current regulations. It would be necessary to provide an enlarged stage, a new fly-tower, new dressing rooms and back stage facilities, new foyers, bars, lavatories and front-of-house accommodation.

The auditorium, the report continued, would merely require repair and renovation but heating, ventilation and lighting for the whole building would be essential throughout and a restaurant might be desirable. The capacity of the theatre reseated to modern standards would be approximately half its original, with seating for only six hundred people.

One strong argument for retaining the Opera House as a working theatre was that Scotland had already lost over one hundred of its eighteenth and nineteenth century theatres. Of all building types that have played a significant role in the community - castles, churches, schools and theatres - the theatre has suffered most.

Only fourteen theatres survive which retain auditoria from the pre-talkie era, including Glasgow Citizens' Theatre, Edinburgh Lyceum Theatre, Theatre Royal Glasgow, Perth Theatre, Pavilion Theatre Glasgow, Gaiety Ayr, King's Theatre Glasgow, King's Theatre Edinburgh, Her Majesty's Aberdeen, and the Tivoli Theatre Aberdeen.

From this it can be seen that the Dunfermline Opera House was a rare theatre. Apart from Perth, it was the only old theatre to survive intact outside Glasgow, Edinburgh and Aberdeen. The importance of the Opera House is increased when the significance of its history after 1900 is understood.

The remodelling of the interior by Swanston in 1921 resulted in an auditorium that was well balanced, retaining all the warmth and intimacy of an earlier age with none of the coarseness of detailing of later, and much larger, movie palaces such as The Playhouse Edinburgh which was built in 1928 or the contemporary chain of Empires built by Milburn.

Very few theatres were built or rebuilt in Britain between the end of the Great War and the coming of the talkies at the end of the twenties. The fact that the Opera House was remodelled by so competent an architect as Swanston, whose King's Theatre Edinburgh is also exceptional, had resulted in an unusually fine theatre.

The Dunfermline theatre has a character not unlike that of the theatres of Thomas Lamb, the prolific American theatre architect, whose work stretches from the turn of the century to the Depression. The flared elliptical arched *soffit* over the orchestra pit was rare in Britain, part of the rococo language translated so successfully into American twentieth century theatre architecture.

Ironically, therefore, the insertion in 1921 of so fine an auditorium a period when so few theatres were built in Britain, increases rather decreases the interest of this building. Study of the 1900 drawings suggest that the original auditorium was not so fine an example of its period.

In the nineteen eighties, many old buildings were being re-assessed, especially those which served the community. This was partly a reaction against the more brutal and inhuman aspects of much of modern architecture, and against the apparently efficient modern auditoria with their good sight lines, fine acoustics and wide stages. These impersonal theatres turned out to have none of the vibrant warmth and close actor-audience contact of most older theatres. Actors and audiences discovered that you laugh more easily, possibly cry more readily in an old theatre than in some of the more featureless cinema-like modern ones.

How are the mighty fallen

Theatre goers and performers prefer a good old auditorium to an indifferent new one. However, the support areas backstage, and also the public areas outside the auditorium of a new theatre, are invariably preferable to the cramped staircases and inadequate lavatories of an old theatre. For many, therefore, the ideal combination would be an old auditorium within a new building.

The report concluded that the Opera House must be worth saving because of the rarity and quality of its auditorium, which was good enough not only to be saved for Dunfermline, but for Scotland and indeed for the whole fabric of British theatre.

The citizens of Dunfermline Town, and of the surrounding district would count themselves lucky in future years when they enjoyed the sort of entertainment a theatre as good as the Opera House could provide.

The auditorium was deemed to be as suitable for popular entertainment, variety, pantomime and rock music, as for drama, opera or ballet. In 1921 a projection box was installed and so the theatre could also serve as an occasional cinema. This could have been significant as the town's five commercial cinemas would eventually close one by one.

An unusual interim use was proposed for the theatre should it be saved without the funds being available for immediate restoration. The Scottish Theatre Company, whose remit was to serve the whole nation, was interested in using the theatre as a production base for the final stage of preparing their productions prior to national tours.

If, as seemed possible, a relatively small expenditure would be needed to arrest decay, and to bring the stage back into use for rehearsal purposes ,(compared with a considerably larger expenditure to bring the whole building into public use) then this offer from a regular tenant would provide a unique opportunity.

Dunfermline had a fine concert hall, The Carnegie Hall, but it had few of the facilities of a well appointed theatre: proscenium arch, flies, orchestra pit or fixed raked seating on multi-levels.

A renovated Opera House would in no way have been a threat to the Carnegie Hall; it could be complementary and allow the town to present the whole range of entertainment to the citizens of both town and region.

Both venues were well positioned relative to the new bus station, car parks and the railway station, so the two could serve what was highly populated region, making Dunfermline a regional centre for entertainment and the arts.

The Dunfermline Opera House could also have had great significance in a national strategy for the performing arts. As the cost of travelling great distances increased it would become necessary to provide theatre in the Lowlands outside of Glasgow and Edinburgh.

There was only one theatre between the two cities and south of Perth which had a fly tower and other important features of a fully equipped conventional theatre. This was the MacRobert Centre, which had problems of access other than by private car because of its situation in a rural university complex outside Stirling.

The Opera House could have been the missing link in the chain of provision for the performing arts in Central Scotland, and as a link in the chain, the Opera House might expect a regular pattern of visits from the national companies commensurate with the scale and size of the theatre, just as the Opera and Ballet Companies regularly visited the Perth Theatre with appropriate items from their repertoire.

There was no doubt that the Scottish Art Council could co-ordinate a presentation of future strategy for the use of the Opera House by major national companies.

Similarly it would also be possible for the Director of Recreation and the Manager of Indoor Halls and Entertainment to indicate the full spectrum of entertainment and of community arts which they would be able to present for the benefit of the citizens of town and region if they had at their disposal the resources of both the Carnegie Hall and of the Opera House.

The Opera House was well situated. In the fifties and sixties preference was given to green field sites with private car parks well outside the city centre. Examples of such theatres include the MacRobert Centre, Stirling.

However experience indicated that, except in exceptional 'festival' circumstances, in Pitlochry for example, the divorce of the theatre from the centre of the town also distances the theatre from the community, emphasising the elitist nature of some of the performing arts.

At the same time city and town centres have tended to become empty in the early evening: when shoppers and office workers leave, the vandals and muggers take over.

There was a good argument, therefore, for rein-stating the arts and especially the performing arts which draw an audience back in the city centre. The arts re-establishes its relationship with the community and popular culture while the developer and planner gain an extension of life into the evening for their centre.

Teenagers are offered something to experience right there in the centre, next to the record shop, with the result that they will find the arts much more accessible than if they were elegantly housed in a park outside the centre. Commercial gains have also proved substantial.

The best site for a theatre from everybody's point of view was now agreed to be the City Centre in the commercial zone, provided that the site is also well positioned for rail and bus travel as well as having available car parks, which can be used by shoppers in the day and theatregoers in the evening. It would also improve the attractiveness of the area as a tourist centre.

Consent for demolition of buildings of special historic or architectural interest should be given only in exceptional circumstances, for example if it they are structurally unsafe and public safety is at risk. This was not a point at issue.

The proposals by the developer for the new James Street shopping centre was for three retail stores and thirty shopping units, all opening off a central mall. It was to be situated next to the proposed new bus station and a car park for five hundred and fifty cars.

The end of another old song...

Left: smoke damage does not altogether hide the beauty of the of carvings
Right: its full beauty is restored

Spotlights replace the Gainsborough lady, and she is given a new home

The detail above the boxes is faithfully reproduced

The beauty of the cherubs shines through the dust of years ...and is now enhanced by sympathetic lighting

Section of the old dress circle… and the new auditorium

The sad and deserted theatre ... now restored to its full glory

A simple memorial in Dalmeny Churchyard to John Henry Hare.

All the credit for the refurbishment of the Opera House in 1921 has been given to the architect J.W Swanston and very little attention paid to the role played by Hare. It was Hare's knowledge of theatres and the entertainment business that showed him the necessity of a modern fully equipped theatre, and that inspired him to employ Swanston. Without John Henry Hare, there would never have been an Opera House as we know it today

Plans for the new shopping centre took no account of the existence of the Opera House and actually cut off part of the frontage. The theatre site was allocated to a department store which was to be the 'magnet' of the development, at the opposite end of the mall from the principal entrances.

This was standard practice in developments of this kind and was designed to encourage customers to walk past as many shops as possible on their way to their principal destination.

No consideration appears to have been given to integrating the Opera House into the development. This practice, common in America, was seen as an additional incentive to use the shopping complex.

It had been successfully achieved in small towns in England and on a much larger scale in the outstandingly successful developments like the Eaton Centre in Toronto and other centres in North America and Australia.

The upgrading of the town centre was necessary so, if the building couldn't be saved, it was necessary to find a way to preserve the interior of the Opera House, one of Dunfermline's unique assets.

It would have been possible to integrate the auditorium completely within the proposed commercial development. The James Street Planning brief stated that there should be a restaurant or boulevard cafe and this could have been integrated with the foyer of the theatre.

An alternative would be to dismantle the existing auditorium piece by piece, taking plaster casts where necessary, and re-erect it with a new stage and ancillary accommodation elsewhere or adjacent to the James Street site. A most successful precedent for this option existed in the demolition and reconstruction of the Lyric Theatre, Hammersmith. Built in 1895 by Frank Matcham, it closed in 1965 and was taken down in 1972 by the specialist firm, George Jackson & Sons, to make way for a commercial development.

Following a public enquiry in 1970-71 the Minister had ruled that the development could take place only if the auditorium was saved for future use. On October 18th, 1979, the reborn Lyric was opened by Her Majesty The Queen on a new site built over a two-level shopping centre. Only the auditorium was re-created, everything else being new and a great improvement on the original ramshackle building.

A third option was to dismantle the existing auditorium, and retain the whole in packing cases for subsequent re-erection somewhere else in Dunfermline or dispose of it to another town in Scotland, England or North America.

The 1980s cost of dismantling and safe storage of the details of the auditorium, based on the known precedent of the Lyric Theatre, Hammersmith, would have cost between forty and seventy thousand pounds.

It appeared that The District Council had already made up its mind. The Director of Planning presented a report which said that much of the original building and its plaster decoration remained intact but 'the general condition of the building is poor, and rain water, penetrating both roof and walls, has done considerable damage.'

The cost of controlling any further decay was estimated at half a million pounds and mothballing the building would cost as much again.

They claimed that the Arts Council study ignored the capital costs of acquiring the building and no organisation had come forward with firm funding proposals to retain the building in its original use. The suggestion that the building be integrated into a new shopping development was dismissed. Its retention would make the development of shopping centre, car park and bus station impossible.

A list of capital projects had already been approved and some would have to be removed to make way for any Opera House project. Besides, West Fife now had two theatres, Lochgelly Centre and Carnegie Hall.

Because The Opera House was purpose built for the production of plays and would give a much more intimate atmosphere, it would represent a financial risk to these. The theatre had closed in 1955 because of the lack of support and councillors argued that people could have come forward with objections any time in the last twenty three years.

There is a certain lack of logic to this. As long as the building was the property of James Bell and Sons and its continued use as workshops agreed by the council, the possibility of public protest was not just limited, it was non-existent. Protest had not availed when the application for change of use had been made.

There is a definite change of tone in newspaper reporting from this stage on. Delay by the Scottish Secretary in making a decision about the future of The Opera House is seen as a threat to the town's development The land holdings of the Regional and District Councils in James Street were to be transferred to Crudens for the redevelopment, who undertook to complete the shopping centre and to co-operate with the Regional Council in the construction of a the car park and bus station.

The success of the work depended on receipt of 'early' planning permission. Any delay could have an effect on other projects in the region's five year plan and they were determined to press ahead with the scheme as quickly as possible. A shopping centre was high on the list of Dunfermline's priorities and Mr George Younger had delayed the granting of permission to Cruden Developments Ltd to demolish the theatre by intervening in the issue of listed building consent.

In October 1981, Provost Les Wood was complaining that the Council had been trying for nine years to bring about this much needed shopping centre.

'A lot of people have been waiting a long time to enjoy the benefits which this complex will bring to the town,' he is quoted as saying, 'and it is frustrating to think it is being held up by people who do not belong to the town and as conservationists, only have a limited interest.'

The Secretary of State for Scotland was accused of dragging his feet on a decision. A St Andrews House spokesman said that Mr Younger was simply taking more time to consider the matter because of the special significance of the building. An impassioned plea was made to Mr Younger in an open letter from district councillor Reverend Douglas Aitken.

Among the points he made were that 'the pressure to retain the Opera House came from organisations outside Dunfermline; the proposals for renovation were such that everything that transforms a building into a theatre required to be replaced.'

It was, he claimed, the ugliest building in the town, was in terrible shape and positively dangerous in places. The people of Dunfermline wanted a shopping centre; they had not stormed the City Chambers in protest at the theatre's removal; if the Opera house were saved, it would have to be subsidised forever out of the rates.

The Opera House 'debacle', as a newspaper headline described it, was a topic which ran and ran. The time table for delivery of Dunfermline's long awaited shopping centre was 1984.

'The date may be significant,' a spokesman for the Dunfermline and West Fife Chamber of Commerce declared, 'for all sorts of miraculous changes were predicted by George Orwell for that particular year.'

At least half a dozen starting and finishing dates had been proposed, and requests for information on availability and terms for leases in the proposed development had received little or no response.

The Director of the Chamber of Commerce felt that too much emphasis had been placed on the St James Street project, and not enough consideration given to proposals for developments at the west end of the town.

They were unconvinced about the merits of siting the bus station beside a major shopping development on the north east periphery of the traditional town centre.

By the beginning of December 1981, six months after first considering the future of the Opera House, Mr Younger still had made no decision.

Provost Wood again complained that an important development, one that would breathe new life into the town and provide jobs for the hard pressed construction industry, was being held up.

In August, the Scottish Secretary had urged local authorities to make swift and sound decisions particularly where major developments were involved, and Provost Wood wished that Mr Younger would take a leaf out of his own book.

Two weeks later, the Provost's wish was granted. Mr Younger decided not to intervene and the demolition of the Opera House could go ahead. He rejected an eleventh hour proposal by a newly formed organisation to save the theatre.

Dick Mehta, secretary of The Friends of the Opera House told The Dunfermline Press that the report prepared by the Scottish Arts Council created such a surge of feeling among local residents that the society was formed with the object of restoring the theatre to a general purpose music hall.

The Chairman of the Friends was Murray Grigor, the film director, who lived in Inverkeithing and had the support of many theatrical and art personalities, many of whom had performed at the Opera House in the past.

Within a week of the society's formation a petition with signatures of one hundred and fifty people living in the Dunfermline area was sent to George Younger.

His decision came as a bitter disappointment to them. In his letter to the District Council, The Secretary of State said that listed buildings such as the Opera House should be retained until it had been demonstrated 'beyond all possible doubt that possibilities of continued use do not exist.'

He had considered all the objections carefully but had regard for the considerable uncertainty about the building being restored and used as a live theatre. Ironically, George Younger, by then Lord Younger, was to be the first chairman of The Edinburgh Festival Theatre from 1991 till his death in 2002. The theatre had survived for many years as a bingo hall before its transformation into a festival centre piece.

Younger's decision to allow the demolition of the Opera House was made on the clear understanding that the council would pursue, with the developer and other interested parties, the possibility of dismantling, storing and re-using elsewhere the theatre's important interior architectural features. Cruden Developments Ltd and The Scottish Arts Council agreed a salvage operation.

Cruden would assist with the cost of re-siting or removing parts of the building up to a maximum of sixty thousand pounds provided a scheme could be drawn up and completed within a six months period.

Law and Dunbar-Nasmith were appointed architects for the restoration project, and were to oversee the work on behalf of the Arts Council, and in consultation with Theatre Projects Consultants.

Harry McCann, Director of the Scottish Arts Council, was disappointed that the Opera House had not been saved in its entirety but was grateful for Cruden's offer of finance.

The building would be demolished but not before substantial parts of the interior, in particular, the impressive auditorium, was surveyed in great detail and the decorative plaster work preserved.

The next problem to be faced was where to find a safe place to store the material. Dunfermline District Council had confirmed that there was no possibility of even a proportion of the material being used in the shopping centre, because of the extra expense that would involve.

The Arts Council would have liked the important architectural features to be housed near their original position, but were now planning to acquire a large storage container.

It would be difficult to find a building big enough to house the artifacts and the container could be easily stored out of doors, perhaps in a secure yard.

It was hoped work would begin soon. Architects were to lay out plans of the pieces as they were brought down so it would be easier for a future developer to reconstruct the jigsaw.

A new twist appeared in the story in May 1982. The Scottish Arts Council were keeping their fingers crossed that their sixty thousand pound plan to save the interior architecture of the Opera House had not gone up in smoke.

The theatre building went on fire early in the evening of Saturday, May 15th. The electricity supply had been cut off so an accidental outbreak was unlikely .

Luckily, the fire station was just across the road in Carnegie Drive and engines were soon on the scene.

Reinforcements came from as far away as Burntisland, and the blaze was brought under control. The fire had taken hold in the wooden beams of the balcony and spread quite rapidly, and a lot of the flooring had to be taken up.

Apart from a certain amount of smoke damage, however, the unique and quite irreplaceable interior of the Opera House escaped lightly. The ornate ceiling and the stage were undamaged. One of the fireman said, that 'although firemen get the reputation of being something of Philistines, even a lay person like myself could see why people wanted to save it. Even when fighting the blaze we could still appreciate its faded splendour.'

To all intents and purposes, Fife's only variety theatre was dead. But if it was, it steadfastly refused to lie down .

Smoke and water from firemen's hoses blur the outlines of the theatre building

TELEPHONE No. 363 DUNFERMLINE.

NEW OPERA HOUSE

REFORM STREET, DUNFERMLINE.

Proprietor and Manager   -   -   -   HENRY HARE.

Monday and Satur., Twice Nightly, at 7 and 9
Tues., Wed., Thurs., Friday, Once Nightly, at 8

PICTURES & VARIETIES

Dress Circle 9d, Stalls & Upper Circle 6d
Pit 4d, Gallery 2d.

DAVID WATT, QUEEN ANNE PRINTING WORKS, DUNFERMLINE

A publicity poster for the Opera House c1929

CHAPTER SEVEN

RENAISSANCE

It was not only the firemen who were impressed by the theatre's fading splendour. Bill Gourlay and Gordon Ellis, members of the recently formed Dunfermline Cine Club, had tried unsuccessfully to get permission from James Bell to photograph the interior.

Having been fascinated by stories of the Opera House, when they heard that demolition was imminent, they wrote to Crudens, the developers, for permission to take what would be the final pictures of a historic building. Permission was duly given, they acquired the keys and began what they originally thought of as a photographic exercise.

Gordon remembered how exciting it was. He had recently moved house and was in the middle of installing a new back door when Bill arrived to tell him he had the keys to the theatre. The job was left half done, the washing machine propped against the door so no-one could get in and they went off to take pictures.

Their equipment was quite primitive by today's standards. To film inside the Opera House they used car headlights powered with a car battery, which they wheeled around on a barrow. It was quite spooky but that added to their excitement.

'From the outside, the theatre was an unattractive building, but inside it was brilliant. It's probably the best venture we've ever done. Once a theatre is demolished, it will never be rebuilt, any new building now will be just a concrete box.

Maybe the acoustics are better but the beauty isn't there. But when you go to an old theatre or cinema...... we went there every night as soon as we'd had our tea, spent more time there than we did at home and went into every hole and corner. I even used to go there in my lunch hour. We used to come out looking like chimney sweeps but it was worth it

We found a cupboard covered up with a sheet of asbestos and took a hammer and screwdriver to get it off, hoping to find something special. All we got was a couple of empty fire buckets. There were bits and pieces lying about, a gas mask, a Capstan cigarette packet and bottles from a local soft drinks firm. Upstairs in one of the attics was a bed, a poster and some fliers. It was quite creepy up there in the attics where the skylights were.

One time, we thought we were the only people in the building, though there could have been others, it was big enough to hide someone in. We heard someone coming in, and footsteps behind the stage curtain. We called out but no-one answered, we're still not sure if anyone was there or not.

We were filming one of the pediments and we never saw a soul. As far as we knew, we had the only key. We still have the key for the shop door, even though the door is long gone.'

Raking about was fun but taking photographs was a serious undertaking. Bell's shop was built in the stalls area and the stage was used as a work shop with heavy electrical power points installed for the machinery. The circle was used as storage space but in spite of this and the years of neglect, the beauty of the original fittings shines through in the photographs. Ornate carvings, ceiling paintings, medallions with representations of Gainsborough ladies were all festooned with heavy fringes of dust.

'We were gobsmacked,' said Bill, 'to Bell it was just a workshop but it was so beautiful, so much more ornate that we expected, considering it had been neglected for over thirty years. When the dismantling began, all the plaster work was cut into sections and placed in what had been the window of Bell's shop.

The ceiling painting couldn't be removed and they tried to reproduce it in Sarasota. A replica was made by a local painter in America but they haven't got it quite right. All the mouldings were removed and the box fronts and doors. The proscenium arch is now wider than it was in The Opera House.'

Bill and Gordon followed the progress of the dismantling and were shocked and dismayed by the fire, which could have put an end to any prospect of the precious plaster work being saved.

They had been in the theatre earlier in the day but had left to take photographs at the cinema in the East Port which was being converted into three cinemas.

A building of such a size was bound to have weak spots where vandals were able to enter but, naturally, as the only people apart from the workmen to have legal access, Bill and Gordon came under suspicion. They were soon able to prove that fire raising in the theatre was the very last thing they wanted.

'Two things saved the Opera House from destruction' said Bill. 'The first was that the fire station was just across the road almost, so firemen could be on the scene very quickly; the second was that when the building was rebuilt in 1921, all the timbers were fireproofed. Top marks to John Henry Hare for that piece of foresight.

We were surprised we were still allowed in after the fire because it was dangerous, especially the area near the refreshment room. I nearly went through the floor at one point. I was walking backwards, looking up, and nearly walked into a ten foot drop.

The vandals had smashed beautiful wood partitions but we have drawings of the rows of the balcony and Gordon has one of the seats. Its cover is past its best but it gives you an idea of the ironwork and the beautiful mahogany edgings. We managed to salvage some bits of plasterwork from the ceiling, and letters that had been row markers.

Crudens weren't interested in the Opera House, they just wanted the site cleared and George Younger, the Secretary of State, wasn't interested either. He came across and put on a pair of overalls to inspect the building, which was listed but he wasn't interested in preserving it, seeing only an old falling down theatre.'

Gordon recalled the day the Opera House was demolished.

'I was having a long lie when my in-laws arrived and told me work had started. I was up like a shot and got some film, which made the basis of a pretty good video. We used Super 8 film which was difficult to work with, but we were fairly new as a group and it was all we had at the time.

Jimmy Logan was very helpful when we made the film. He was delighted to talk to us, and narrated part of the soundtrack one time when he was doing a show in the Adam Smith Halls in Kirkcaldy. He had been a juvenile lead in his early days and appeared at the Opera House with his Mum and Dad.

He told us he had his heart set on buying it but didn't have the money at the time. He knew the place inside out, talked about the boxes, pit, flies, the entrances for the refreshment room and all the other parts of the building that we had already seen and could recognise from his story.

Altogether we spent three years researching and making a twenty minute film *Dunfermline Opera House 1903 – 1983* which won seven awards, including The Pilgrim Trust Award. We were delighted as it had never come to Dunfermline before.

There had been talk at one time of the Opera House being incorporated into the new shopping centre, but that was always a non-starter. Luckily the Scottish Arts Council were interested in preserving the building.

They saw it as a very important theatre interior, with very few places like it except maybe the Gaiety in Ayr and the Perth Theatre. That's how the interior of the building was saved.

It was like a big jigsaw puzzle and all the pieces were packed into a big container which ended up in a yard in Elgin Street Industrial Estate.

When we applied to Crudens in March 1982 for permission to take photographs, they wrote to us, enclosing the key for the door in Carnegie Street. They also sent a copy of their letter to Sir James Dunbar– Nasmith in Edinburgh. He got in touch with us and we took about two hundred photos across to Edinburgh for him to see.

He was keen on theatres, he'd been involved in building the Eden Court Theatre in Inverness and had done a number of restoration jobs. He and the Scottish Arts Council were trying to find a buyer for the listed interior and he put a portfolio together.

These were the photos that the people from Sarasota saw and as well as the pieces of the interior which had all been numbered, they had our photographs to work from so a near replica could be made.

Sir James Dunbar-Nasmith, at that time Professor of Architecture at Edinburgh College of Art, was one of the prime movers in the story of the renaissance of the Opera House.

He had been involved in the building and restoration of several theatres including The Eden Court Theatre in Inverness, The Festival Theatre in Berwick, the Theatre Royal, Glasgow and the Birmingham Hippodrome.

He worked closely with theatre consultant, Iain Mackintosh, whose firm have offices in London and New York, and who was involved in theatre building in America.

They had worked together on *Curtains!!! or A New Life For Old Theatres*, a comprehensive gazetteer which listed all the theatres and music halls built in Great Britain before 1914, and noted whether they still survived as theatres or were being used for other purposes.

The Opera House was, of course, included and the entry concludes: 'As one of the most attractive medium sized theatres in Scotland, its retention and return to its original purpose is highly recommended.'

Sir James and Iain Mackintosh fought together to save the Opera House from demolition, had written the Scottish Arts Council report which is detailed in chapter six but, in spite of their best efforts, the proposed shopping mall won the day and the theatre was doomed.

'It really was completely unnecessary to demolish it,' said Sir James, 'It would only have cost peanuts to retain it but nobody at that time felt there was a future for it. Yet the Perth Theatre, designed by the same architect, around the same time, shows how successfully it could have been renovated.'

Partial victory was gained, however, with the agreement that the interior be saved though, at the time, they had no notion whether it would ever see the light of day again.

Leonard Grandison, and his firm of ornamental plasterers from Peebles, was entrusted with the task of removing the ornate fibrous plasterwork.

After a photogrammetric survey, which recorded where the pieces were to go, box fronts, cornices and friezes were carefully dismantled, numbered and catalogued, wrapped in towelling and packed in a container.

For more than three years, the container lay in a council yard, more or less forgotten while other battles were fought, and other contracts fulfilled. Then one day, Iain Mackintosh received a phone call from David Staples, a colleague in Sarasota.

The Asolo Theatre Company wanted to move from their tiny little Italian court theatre, which had been imported from Asolo in Italy, into something a little bigger.

In a way, history was repeating itself. On a visit to Venice in 1949, A. Everett Austin, director of the John and Mable Ringling Museum of Art, stumbled across some crates containing the eighteenth century Asolo theatre.

It was bought by the museum as an addition to their collection of eighteenth century art and the crates spent the next couple of years hidden from view in the museum's basement.

In 1952, it was installed in the museum's gallery 21, where it played a double role as an art object and the museum's lecture hall. The first production by the Florida state University Art Department took place there in 1953.

Five years later, a new building had been constructed to house the Asolo, and it became the home of a summer theatre company founded by Florida State University in 1960.

It developed into a year round professional theatre, and eventually the F.S.U. Asolo Conservatory, but it was too small for the purpose and by the 1980s, plans were going ahead a new state of the art theatre. Nearly a third of the money for the project was provided by the state, and the rest was raised locally in less than four years.

Plans for the new theatre complex were supported by, among others, Burt Reynolds, who donated one million dollars. He had studied at Florida State University Theatre school, and wanted Asolo to provide, as well as a theatre, a sound stage where plays could be taped for cable television.

At the same time, the directors wanted a theatre space, connected in spirit to the classic European style of the original Asolo.

The management were worried about the audience reaction to being asked to leave an intimate little three hundred and eighteen seat theatre for a modern building seating five hundred, so the news that exactly what they wanted did exist must have seemed almost a miracle.

David Staples, a theatre consultant, was asked for help in building larger premises, and he knew that his colleague Iain Mackintosh had campaigned to save the Dunfermline Opera House, and was partly responsible for the preservation of its unique interior.

Staples' phone call was to ask if the 'theatre in a packing case' still existed. Mackintosh immediately phoned Sir James who checked the container, and then contacted the Scottish Arts Council, which was responsible for it.

The firm which had carried out the dismantling of the Opera House auditorium were worried about how much longer the pieces could survive.

Dunfermline didn't want it and could envisage no possible use for it, so the Asolo committee were told that it was still there and available.

The Scottish Arts Council did make some stipulations, however. Dunfermline was to receive a small donation, possibly to be spent on improvements to the Carnegie Hall; the *Curtains !!!* project would also receive a donation towards a second edition; and the pieces in the container were to be treated with care and affection.

Three consultants were to be appointed, who would travel to Sarasota to check the rebuilding was carried out precisely according to plan and that no unjustifiable alterations would be made.

Before this happened, however, Elizabeth Lindsay, a board member of the Asolo Theatre, came to Edinburgh with her family during the Edinburgh Festival.

Sir James remembered picking her up at the Caledonian Hotel, dressed very fetchingly in a white boiler suit.

When they reached Dunfermline, Sir James expected Mrs Lindsay to have a quick look inside the container. Instead, Mrs Lindsay, who had trained as an architect, crawled inside with a torch and made a proper inspection.

'Even in the container, we could see it was just what we wanted,' she said later, when the theatre was completely rebuilt, 'We could have had a modern theatre but the people of Sarasota didn't want a box, they wanted a proper theatre that was warm and intimate.

We couldn't have created this ambience, even by copying it. It is warm, friendly and inviting. What inspired me to bring the Scottish theatre to Florida was the sight of one of the box fronts upside down in the van.'

That inspiration resulted in a new chapter in theatre history being written. It was only the third theatre interior ever to be dismantled and rebuilt in its entirety.

During the second world war, the the Cuvillies theatre in Munich, in which Mozart is said to have played, was dismantled and rebuilt again in the fifties.

In 1979, the Lyric Theatre, Hammersmith was rebuilt near its original site. According to Iain

Mackintosh, cities have always torn down their theatres in the name of reform.

'People say modern is good. A successful town demolishes its theatres, an unsuccessful town keeps theirs. All the best old theatres are in towns that aren't as rich as they used to be.'

Buildings had been exported before but, apart from the fragments of the earlier Asolo building, the Opera House was the first theatre to cross the Atlantic, travelling four thousand miles to its new home, and arriving in America just before Christmas 1986.

But it had not been sent out alone into the world. Three consultants had been appointed to take care of it : Sir James Dunbar-Nasmith, Iain Mackintosh and Leonard Grandison, who with his son, had dismantled the plasterwork in Dunfermline. For three years they represented the Scottish Arts Council, and were responsible for overseeing the work carried out by architect Stuart Barger and his team of craftsmen.

The reconstruction of the plaster work was difficult for the Americans. The two box fronts had each been removed in one piece, but the rest of the plaster work details had to be applied in situ, and the bombé curve to the front of the dress circle proved difficult. Ian Mackintosh remembered instructing the master plasterer to try and give it 'a bit more Dolly Parton and the finished job was exactly as Iain wanted it.

The warm Dunfermline colour scheme was not suitable for Florida so American and Scots devised an eau de nil, green, gold and scarlet combination . A Scottish thistle over the stage right box is balanced by Florida orange blossoms on the left. The

firm they used specialised in the restoration of churches theatres and other public buildings.

According to Iain Mackintosh, they were 'simply the best' and the finished result, a new five hundred seat theatre, was superior to any of the restorations he had worked on in Britain.

The Opera House, now known as The Esther M. and Harold E. Mertz Theatre, is part of The Asolo Center For Performing Arts.

The three storey building, costing fourteen million dollars, also contains a laboratory theatre, classrooms and rehearsal rooms for Florida State University students, a television studio and technical facilities for the university's Conservatory of Motion Picture, Television and Recording Arts.

Some alterations had to be made. The new proscenium arch is four feet wider than the original, and eighty per cent of the ornamentation was recast in Sarasota from moulds made from the originals shipped from Scotland. The beautiful box fronts with their painted cherubs are now enhanced by sympathetic lighting .

'The blend of the old and the new is seamless,' Sir James told the Sarasota Herald Tribune in 1989, 'it's a marvellous restoration job.'

Sir James was delighted with the success of the whole project. 'It was sad that we couldn't keep the Opera House standing in Dunfermline, but if it had to come down, it's wonderful that it's going to get a new life.'

That new life began officially in January 1990, when Burt Reynolds and his wife Loni Anderson were in the audience for the gala opening. After the performance of Shaw's *Man and Superman*, the film star cut the ribbon for the centre's film and television wing which is named after him. He said he wanted to do some teaching and was hoping to help with student film productions. Another honoured guest was Esther M. Mertz, after whom the theatre was named.

In a city settled by Scots, it was fitting that the ceremonies should include a pipe band and highland dancers from Riverview High School in Sarasota.

Apart from Burt Reynolds, most plaudits went to Elizabeth Lindsay. As well as visiting Dunfermline and giving her seal of approval to 'the theatre in a packing case,' she was responsible for raising more than half the money needed for the project.

Hardly surprising then, that the Herald Tribune described her as beaming when she looked around at the glittering audience, also enjoying the play. 'She was,' they said, 'wearing a gown the colour of rich Burgundy wine, accented by a sash of Lindsay plaid draped from shoulder to waist.'

John Ulmer, the artistic director said that it was a miracle - 'an honest to God certified miracle.'

State Senator Bob Johnson, a member of the Asolo Board, called the new centre 'the greatest building in the world' and 'a monument to co-operation.'

Jim Scheurenbrand, First Florida regional executive vice president, was quoted as saying. 'When I see the people who are here and think of all the thousands of people to follow... it makes it all worthwhile. This building and everything in it will last for generations. It's for everybody, not an elitist crowd.'

What an epitaph for the Opera House. It was always everybody's palace of entertainment. From the local dignitaries in their boxes, the merchants in the dress circle, to the shop assistants, miners and labourers in the gallery, it united everyone in innocent enjoyment.

Like the prophet, the Opera House was without honour in its own country, but in Sarasota, they realised its worth and regarded it as a jewel in their crown.

Among the honoured guests at the gala night in Sarasota was James Cameron, Provost of Dunfermline.

'I didn't take office till long after the Opera House had been demolished,' he told a reporter, 'but faced with the same dilemma, I think I would have made the same decision. My predecessor said that if the 1812 Overture had been played in the Opera House, the building would have fallen down.'

Cameron and Timothy Mason, the Director of the Scottish Arts Council travelled to Sarasota with Professor James Dunbar–Nasmith and Lorna Blackie, a reporter with *The Glasgow Herald.*

'It was a terrible night,' Cameron recalled, 'very stormy. Our plane was one of the last to get out of Gatwick that night, we were lucky to get out with the high winds. The Professor picked up a car at the airport and took us to a hotel in Sarasota.

The heat was terrific. The dedication ceremony was on January 27th and the sun was sweltering down, the temperature was in the eighties and we were dressed in suits, collars and ties. There were choirs of singers, the Kilties pipe band played and the Highlanders did the sword dance. Timothy Mason and I were made Freemen of the City of Sarasota, and my name is still there on the brass plaque.

For the play at might, James Dunbar-Nasmith suggested we wear kilts to bring a bit of Scotland into it. Timothy Mason and I cut ribbons and made speeches and mingled with the stars.

Mrs Mertz was there. She had donated five million dollars so the theatre could be named after her late husband.'

In his speech, Timothy Mason said that it was rather a sad occasion for Scotland, which had lost the Opera House forever, but as in a fairy tale the sleeping beauty could now go to the ball.

Iain Mackintosh recalled the ceremony as very moving.

'The dignitaries assembled on a bright sunny day outside the theatre. The mayor granted the freedom of Sarasota to James Cameron and Tim Mason, who made a witty speech.

Burt Reynolds, a principal donor and alumnus of Florida State university, with which the Asolo is closely associated, was late.

A local kilted pipe band played *Scotland the Brave*. I wept. The Provost had a ride in the longest stretch limo in Florida, the property of million dollar donor Esther E. Mertz, after whose late husband the auditorium was to be named.

We all had a wonderful time. What the whole project had proved was that it was possible for old theatres to be given a new lease of life, though export should always be the last resort, to be considered only if the alternative is destruction.

In spite of the huge complexity of the problem of dismantling and transplanting the Opera House interior, from both the technical and aesthetic view, it has proved that removal and reconstruction is not only feasible but practical.

If commercial pressures dictate that some gorgeous palace be dissolved to 'leave not a rack behind,' the technology and skills have now been developed to beam it down elsewhere.'

Plaster and woodwork worth preserving

CHAPTER EIGHT

YES I REMEMBER IT WELL

Over the years, many Dunfermline people have made sentimental journeys to Florida.

Frank and Margaret Tait visited Sarasota in 1993, and were very keen to take a trip to see the old Dunfermline Opera House in its new home at the Asolo Center for the Performing Arts.

Frank was in the process of retiring from his post as Depute Director of Administration with Dunfermline District Council, and had written from the City Chambers to Sarasota to say that he would be on holiday in Florida and that he and his wife would like to visit the Centre. They were warmly welcomed by two of the Directors and given the grand tour of the theatre.

'The entrance foyer was not at all as it had been in Dunfermline,' Margaret recalled, ' but the moment we stepped into the auditorium, it was as if someone had transported us back in time.

Certainly, the colours were different to the old Opera House, but the lay-out, the style of the seats, the metal seat ends, the carving on the boxes, plasterwork, and so much more, were all exact replicas.

The proscenium was much larger but copied perfectly, and even the curtains and pelmet were exactly right, apart from the decoration which had been given gold decorative symbols from Florida in place of the Scottish ones.

Normally I am not a particularly sentimental person, but I have to say I had a lump in my throat as memories of my childhood came flooding back of the good old days in Dunfermline Opera House.'

Andy Hamilton's visit was in 2000.

'As International Commissioner of Scouts for Fife, I was a guest at the American National Jamboree in which thirty five thousand scouts were taking part. I was staying with a federal judge in Tampa, who had been to the Boy Scouts jamborette at Blair Castle in 1999.

I was taken to the Mayor's office, presented with a book, and shown round the Ringling Brother's Museum and The Opera House. I stood on the stage at the Asolo and reminisced.

My sister Sally and I were both members of Helen Millar's dancing class in the forties and in 1945 we were chosen to appear for a week at The Opera House.

Aged about ten and twelve, we shared the stage with Jack Fuller and Jimmy Lang, doing one show a day during the week and two on Saturday. We didn't get paid because we were under age, but Arthur Lax presented my sister with a bouquet.

The Opera House was always a major part of our lives. We used to go every Saturday with Mum and Dad. We'd start queuing for the second house as soon as the first house went in, and we'd race in and up the stairs so we would get the front seats in the gods. After I started work, I used take Mum every week as a thank you for taking us. We sat in the first and second seats in the stalls. With my first pay, I treated Mum to a box. When I went to Asolo, I was able to stand in that box once again. It was wonderful to see the theatre resurrected.'

Ken and Barbara Logan went to Sarasota in October 2002, and their visit to the Opera House was organised by Dunfermline expatriate Jack Romanes.

'The whole place is a marvellous big estate, about twice the size of Pittencrieff park,' Barbara said, 'and there are little buggies to take you from place to place. An arts museum is based in what was a mansion belonging to the Budweiser family, which has its own jetty made of pink marble. We could never imagine the Opera House in this setting.

'When I saw the building I didn't think it could be the Opera House because it was so huge. We were thinking of the narrow streets and the long Saturday night queues, while here was an enormous foyer with a Yamaha grand piano and a lovely, peaceful atmosphere. When they opened the door to the theatre, though, I felt the hairs on the back of my neck begin to rise. It was like stepping back in time.'

Ken was equally amazed. 'The fascia of the theatre complex bears no relationship to the Opera House, it's such a great expanse of building. Go through the doors though and it's there, just as it used to be.

I had always wanted to sit in one of the boxes and now I got my wish. They've done it proud. The whole thing, the little sitting room off the box, the replica seats, even the lighting was the same.

Apparently some of the original fittings were salvaged and copied to make them authentic The curtains were the same too. It was just like being back in the past, with the Opera House in all its glory and we were quite emotional. It was wonderful.

'Susan Melum, the manager of the theatre, couldn't do enough for us, we were given VIP treatment all the way. I told her we were very impressed but they had made one mistake. There was no orchestra pit.

Andy and Sally Hamilton

But it was my mistake. What they have done is to build an extended stage which rolls out over the top of the orchestra pit when it's not required. We were delighted because we have happy memories of Arthur Lax bobbing up and down in that pit.

Among the many memories of our visit, one that stands out is seeing the life size brass rubbing of Robert The Bruce, taken in Dunfermline Abbey.

Theatre is a magic made up of a wide range of ingredients - owners who provide space for the drama to take place, writers and composers whose imagination produces it, musicians in the orchestra pit, craftsmen who provide the scenery and props, backstage staff who make sure the curtain rises and falls on time; actors, comedians, dancers and a whole range of artistes who bring their talents to the stage.

There are the unsung workers, lighting and sound engineers, usherettes, bar and restaurant staff, cleaners and doormen and last but not least the audience, without which none of this would be possible.

Almost fifty years after its curtain came down for the last time, many people still have fond memories of The Opera House.

Elizabeth Cowan was born in Crossgates in 1911 and still remembers her first visit to The Opera House shortly after it reopened in 1921 to see a play performed by The Dunfermline Amateur Dramatic Society.

She was in the Guides at the time and the leader, a teacher at Crossgates School, was a dancer and put on a guide concert every year. Elizabeth recalled one where she took the part of Florence Nightingale and borrowed an apron from the local midwife for a costume. John Henry Hare was in the first farce she went to, but she was more impressed by the Shakespeare and Shaw performances.

When she was older, Elizabeth coaxed her boy friend to take her to the theatre but by then the shows were too expensive.

Kay Burke Craine remembered being taken to the Opera House by her boy friend. 'Boys always had more money than girls in those days and he always bought me a box of chocolates and we sat in the dress circle.'

The best memory for Kay's sister in law, Bunty Lamberton was seeing Ma and Pa Logan with young Jimmy dressed as a schoolboy with short trousers, a blazer and cap. She recalled going with her mother-in-law on Saturday nights and the queues stretching up Pilmuir Street.

The Lambertons went to Clearwater in Florida to visit their nephew and paid a visit to the Asolo. 'We were very lucky. An afternoon show was just coming out and when we told them we were from Dunfermline, they allowed us in.'

Morris Allan remembered one special occasion. When he was about ten, the football team at McLean Primary School, for which he played, had reached the final of the Dick Cup, and their final match ended in a one all draw.

'Our teacher Miss Walker was also our coach and all the boys worshipped her. As a reward for doing so well, she arranged a visit to The Opera House after the game to enjoy a variety show with Charlie Kemble.

One of Charlie's specialities during his long stay at The Opera House, was to compose and sing

Safety curtain with the Stephens advert in the prized centre space

little ditties with news of the day. Picture twelve shining schoolboy faces as Charlie Kemble sang their footballing fame to a house full of patrons, who joined in three cheers for McLean and wished them luck in the replay.

How did he know about us, how did he even know we were in the theatre, let alone know the school's football story? We were absolutely delighted to get a special cheer for Miss Walker and who could blame her if she had a sudden need for a hankie to dry her eyes.

Another surprise was that Charlie came on stage holding the cup aloft, and announced to the company that McLean was to share the trophy with the Cowdenbeath school we had drawn with.'

When he left school, Morris became a cub reporter with the Dunfermline Journal. He got two tickets for the show every week and had to do a write up of the show. Perhaps to ensure a supply of tickets, he never gave adverse criticism.

The fact that Charlie Kemble held the record for the longest continuous appearance at the Opera House probably explains why so many people remember him.

James Matson first saw him when he was about five or six years old. James was sitting in a box at the right hand side of the stage and Charlie did a song and dance about him. Much later, as an electrician with Scotts , James worked the spotlights up in the gods for a time. A framed 1920s style poster giving details of seat prices still hangs on his wall.

Bryan McIver was a lighting engineer for a time.

'I worked there as a "lime" operator graduat-ing from off prompt, prompt, rear of house and finally to the main switchboard controlling the stage and the auditorium lighting. It was during the early 1940s at which time I was serving my apprenticeship as an electrical fitter at Comrie Colliery which was situated between Blairhall and Saline.

This sideline ended when I attained the age where I was required to work underground and on rotational shift work which of course made it impossible to be available for the evening shows.

The "limes" were of the type which used a form of carbon pencil, the lower as thick as a human thumb the upper somewhat thinner and it was necessary to strike an arc to set it going ith continual adjustment to the space between to provided the brilliant white light.

The heat from these units was quite something especially the more powerful unit at the rear of the Auditorium.

The flicker effect when required was intended to be by means of a slide-in mechanism which once in place required the operator to spin a disc to the speed required by the lighting instructions given by the stage manager.

The cumbersome nature of the attachment often led to distracting noise so the operators got a similar effect by the simple expedient of waving their hand in front of the lens.

Joe Plant was the stage manager, Claude Worth the producer. He was very fond of Scotland, especially of Edinburgh and to show his appreciation of the place he dedicated a park bench type seat, complete with plaque, which is still there on Princes Street.

Arthur Lax was Director of Music at that time and Harry Buchanan the lighting switchboard operator. Charley Kemble, Tommy Morgan and Jimmy Lang were popular comedians and The Moxon Girls were a top favourite, and lovely girls they were.

The War was in full swing at this time and people seemed to disappear from time to time having been called up to serve in the armed forces. The leader of the Moxon troop was one such person and her dance training was to her advantage, so much so that when next she paid the theatre a visit some six or eight weeks later she was wearing full corporal stripes.

My wife's grandmother was one of those wonderful landladies who 'put-up' the performers. As a small girl my wife used to see and hear the lodgers practice their acts and she seemingly enjoyed every moment.

Grandmother had the same two seats permanently booked for years for every Friday night performance at the Dunfermline Opera House and never missed a show. On occasion, if one or other of the grandchildren were in favour, they were allowed to accompany her to a show, a great treat.'

Like Bryan, Ken Logan also worked at the Opera House.

'For about three years I helped operate the side lights, the coloured lantern lights which were played down on to the stage. That was interesting because you saw the shows for free. We started about six thirty to get ready for the seven thirty start. The orchestra was under Mr Lax and we'd be talked through the show and given a sheet showing what lights had to be used, and when.

We got five shillings a week, a lot of money for those days but you were expected to be there every night and both shows on a Saturday. That was a killer, and sometimes there was an extra show on a Friday as well.

I can't remember all the artistes. Charlie Kemble stood out, but there were so many, and we were more interested in just operating the lights and getting paid for it. Sometimes we'd go through to the back stage for something to eat.

My other connection with The Opera House involved animals. I was brought up in Ingle street. My grandfather was cattleman at the market there for fifty years.

The Opera House used the cattle market for the livestock they used in shows and in the forties, when I was twelve or thirteen, I got the job of bringing the animals up.

My grandfather had collie dogs which were often used and they were no bother but invariably, during Irish week, it was a big billy goat, a nanny goat, a kid and a donkey.

It was a difficult kettle of fish getting the billy across. He had a rope round his neck and was much stronger than me so he had me running up through the market.

At the market entrance at Ingle Street, there was a pillar between the pedestrian gate and the big ones for the floats. I went round one side of the pillar and he went round the other, then I had to manoeuvre him across the road. To get into the Opera house, there was a close between the chip shop and the pub which took you to what was meant to be a fire exit, but was just a single door, and we went up a long, narrow, passageway and through a side door onto the stage. The animals had to be held there till they were due to go on stage, and sometimes billy amused himself by eating the curtains.

The animals were donated by local farmers and they weren't trained or anything, and they certainly weren't house trained. There were usually messes on the stage which always caused a guffaw or two.

The dogs were no problem but donkeys and goats were. They even tried sheep once, for Bo-Peep I think. You can tell a dog, you can almost tell a goat where you want it to go but a sheep? No it goes its own way.

There was a hue and cry when the Opera House closed first but people soon lost interest. Some of the highlights though - on Saturday nights, especially when there were top notch artistes, the buses couldn't get down Ingle Street. When one house came out and the other was going in, the queues would be right round Reform Street into Pilmuir Street. The sight of the people in Ingle street and Reform Street in summer was something to behold.

They didn't want to go home after the show and would just stand about and blether. There were hundreds of people, the streets choc-a-bloc so you could hardly move.

It seems strange looking back but it was an everyday occurrence to us. Paper sellers on the street and people milling around, that's something that has gone, like the money. I used to get three pence a week for helping my grandfather and that got me a bar of chocolate, a comic and a visit to the pictures.

What I remember most about the Opera House was the quality of the entertainment, the same company doing a twenty week summer season with a change of show every week. When all the cast came on stage at the end of the show it was quite impressive.'

Ken had vivid recollections of the farmers who came to the market, then congregated in the Station Tavern at lunchtime, before going on to a show in the Opera House.

Dave Willis

Harry Govier remembered those farmers. He had many memories of being in the Opera House while it was still a theatre. His father changed scenery and worked the lights. Harry helped him on occasion.

' My father got to know the artistes. Charlie Kemble came to our house in Campbell Street. We usually sat in the gods, but occasionally father sneaked us into the boxes. I remember seeing Will Fyffe and an act with dogs jumping through hoops.

There used to be a wee baker's shop, Ramages, across from the Opera House and nearby was Wise's chip shop. It was always packed on show nights and they would send across fish suppers for people in the show.

Later on, Harry had a closer connection with the Opera House. He was a foreman upholsterer with James Bell and Sons, and when Bell bought the building, he divided it into three workshop areas.

'The showroom was downstairs where the stalls had been, the circle was where everything was stored ready for going into the show room, and the cabinet maker's workshop, with all its saws, planes and heavy machinery, was on the stage.

The first day Bell's went into the building, it was it had always been, but we had to level it off. The gods were on a slope so we took out ten rows of seats to make a level space to work on. We had two levels.'

Harry began with Bells in 1948 and left in 1970 to join the royal household. He worked in Holyrood Palace for thirty years and was awarded the Queen's Personal Medal and a Jubilee Medal.

Brenda Kucharewski also remembers the farmers. Her mother worked in the Tavern and provided the meals, and Brenda would come from Queen Anne School for half an hour at lunchtime to help.

She recalls going to pantomimes at the Opera House and has a fund of memories handed down from her mother. The owner of the pub, Willie Whittle, was friendly with all the stars who came to the theatre.

'My mother used to tell me stories of how she took care of many of the people who performed there. They would come into the pub for a drink, a talk or if they ran out of anything. She kept an emergency store of things, sugar and so on for them.

One story I found specially interesting because I had seen this man perform. My mother used to take me to the theatre in Glasgow in the take me to the theatre in Glasgow in the days of Lex Mclean, and Will Starr would be appearing in some of these variety shows.

Will came into the bar one day in a sorry state, unshaven and having had too much to drink. Mother gave him shaving gear, cleaned him up and fed him cups of coffee and tea to sober him up. He was very popular in the fifties but by the early sixties, his career was ending. I'm sure my mother must have helped many others as well.

When the Tavern was being demolished to make way for the Kingsgate and the new bus station, a whole collection of photographs and posters turned up and I found them when I was clearing out my mother's house after she died. They brought back lots of memories.'

It was the standing ovation at the end of the show that was the brightest memory for Grace Henderson from Saline.

She remembered going to The Opera House in the early forties, when she was about ten. Sandy Scott from Oakley went with his dad and recalled climbing up to the gods with a bag of oranges.

The bag burst and the oranges bounced down the stairs with kids in hot pursuit. Sandy's first and most lasting memory is of the fire curtain, with its beautifully coloured adverts.

George Simmonds was friendly with a number of the stars. 'When I was three or four, I used to go to The Opera House with my grandparents. We had seats booked for Harry Lauder but we were late in getting there and our seats were sold so we got a box.

Later we used to go every Saturday night with Frank Bell. His wife and sister wore little pink coats and Charlie Kemble made up poems about them. The Four Ds were a very popular act, saxophone, piano, accordion and drums. They always insisted on having the same dressing room which had a hatch through to the bar.

I knew Chic Murray very well, met him in Edinburgh one day and invited him back to Dunfermline. Doug Stockdale, a friend of mine, invited Chic as a guest to his silver wedding and Chic agreed as he wasn't expected to speak. The best man, though, decided Chic should take over the speeches. He did and entertained the company in his own inimical fashion.

Aly Wilson was a great favourite. Johnny Mack was his straight man and he always wore a camel coat with a belt. They used to do sketches with the two of them in the same bed and nobody thought anything of it. They wouldn't be able to do it today.'

The romance of the theatre was not always reserved for the stage. Catherine (Irene) Sneddon from Crossgates, whose daytime job was as a machinist with Wilson & Wightman, Pilmuir Street, augmented her pay by working in the evening as an usherette at the Opera House. Her friend Babs Lucas was also an usherette, and Babs' brother worked backstage.

Ian Campbell was a Glaswegian whose family moved to Dunfermline while he was doing his National Service in the R.A.F. He well remembers his first visit to the theatre.

'In early 1954, as demobilisation approached I paid my first visit to the Opera House (my maternal grandparents sang under the baton of Sir Hugh Roberton with the Glasgow Orpheus and Phoenix choirs in the 1920s and, regrettably I only inherited their love of music, not the voice).

I do not remember if it was on that occasion I watched and listened to David Whitfield, but I do remember hearing him sing "Cara Mia Mine".

I attended the Opera House several times and in the early stages was attracted to the young usherette, Irene, as she went about her work. I must have been somewhat obvious as Babs told Irene that I had attended the same show a couple of times and kept looking at her.

The day after I first saw her I went to work and told friends I had seen the girl I wanted to become my wife. When asked by my mother, I had to admit I did not know who she was, only that she had the same beautiful brown eyes as my dog (which was meant as a compliment).

I did manage to get the words to *Cara Mia* and a date with Irene on 5th July that year. We married in 1956 in Canmore Congregational Church and had four sons. Dunfermline Opera House featured largely when we talked with friends and relatives.

My brother-in-law, who was my best man, re-told the story at our Ruby Wedding and I have never ceased to thank what or whoever it was that made me enter the Opera House. I have much to be thankful for in its existence.

For eleven years now, my family and friends have held an annual gathering, mainly in the West of Scotland but also in Ayrshire and Fife. It was held in Baldridgeburn Hall in 1996. While we had an afternoon meal in Dunfermline with friends, we sat near an American couple and, on the spur of the moment, decided to invite them to the gathering, which they gladly accepted.

They were Dick and Penny Garden, and by a strange coincidence, came from Sarasota, Florida, where the interior of the Opera House is now in-stalled within the Asolo State Theatre.'

George McDonald recalled the good old days of entertainment in Dunfermline.

'The Kinema Ballroom - ah, a place you could really dance in, where boy met girl and we would always say *May I have this dance* or even *May I have the pleasure* if it was someone spe-cial. For one shilling and sixpence I danced the night away Monday to Saturdays 7.30 till 10.30.

It certainly was the place to keep fit, with band-leaders Cecil Hunter, Horace Demarco and others, one could enjoy dancing in strict tempo. There was no alcohol in the ballroom in those days, and drugs were only in chemist shops. I really enjoyed my nights at the ballroom.

You could carry on a conversation with your partner without being drowned out by the band, and there was always Cherry, who kept an eye on things. There was no need for bouncers then. Age was no barrier either, as the mix could be sixteen to sixty six and no one felt out of place.

The Opera House, weren't we spoiled in those days for entertainment? I remember Arthur Lax leading the Orchestra and entertainers too numer-ous to mention, and queues right along Reform Street waiting for the next house to start. Even if we could only afford sixpence for the gods, we felt like a million dollars being there.

The Unitas was another great dance hall. Old time and modern, time about, a superb dance floor and a very nice decorative ceiling. The Ice Rink was a better rink than most and I feel for the young people of this town being denied skating facilities.

And then there were the 'Vikings'. What a way to spend a Saturday - to watch the 'Pars' in the af-ternoon and go to see the Vikings at night, espe-cially if both won.

The Regal was a really super picture house, it must have been one of the best in Scotland in its day. The Kinema and the Alhambra both have their memories too and who could forget the cowboys at the Cinema. There were so many bullet holes in the rafters it's a wonder the ceiling didn't come down.

We had two railway stations, two bus stations, two bus depots, a cattle market, tram cars, factories and we even had full employment. In all we had a lot to live for, most people were on an equal foot-ing and demands were not so high.

Bill Findlay remembered the Opera house very well from his childhood days.

'My parents were loosely connected with the theatre and entertainment business. My mother was a dancing teacher and my father a musician. A friend of Arthur Lax, he sometimes stood in for Mr Haldane, the drummer in the orchestra.

I can remember as a very young child being backstage in the Opera House watching the shows from the wings and being fussed up by the chorus girls before I was old enough to appreciate it.

My mother was a friend of May Moxon and also a man and wife dance duo who used to visit us when they performed in Dunfermline but whose names I can't now remember.

On several occasions, two of my mothers senior dancing pupils - Betty Rosetti and Iris McCormak - performed a tap routine on the programme and were very successful but being under age and still at school, they should not have been performing.

Somehow, Mr Alec Elder, the school attendance officer and head of the watch committee, got word of this and the girls had to stay hidden until he had left the theatre.

I can remember Harry Gordon and Will Fyffe. I once played an accordion duet with Will Fyffe's son at the Synod Hall in Edinburgh. My favourite comedian was Tommy Hope. To me he was, and still is, the greatest.

My aunt kept theatrical digs in Buffies Brae and most of the artists visiting Dunfermline stayed with her. I got to know most of the artists who performed at the Opera House during the 1930s and 40s so I have many memories.

I was away doing service with the RAF when the theatre closed. I had grown up with the notion that show business, particularly variety, was my destiny. I was well prepared for it from childhood but by the time I finished my national service in the RAF, show business and variety as we knew it, was over.

I have many happy memories of the Opera House and the people who performed there. Apart from Tommy Hope, my number one favourite I remember so many of the other variety artists, Bobby Telford, another great comedian, Ma and Pa Logan and the Family, Charlie Kemble, and Tommy Lorne. Will Fyfe was a truly great favourite who could create an intimate atmosphere with the audience, and Clark and Murray.

Then of course, there was Alec Finlay (no relation) a real gentleman whom I knew personally and had many pleasant chats with.

There are so many others who slip my memory but there was Willie Wallace, an amateur who based himself on George Robey, and a three legged soldier who marched about the stage doing comical antics. I'm not sure, but I think it was Billy Dainty who did this three legged turn − long before Rolf Harris's three legged Jake.

I absolutely adored conjurers and illusionists. I remember the Great Levante his daughter Esme, and Horace Goldin. I was never allowed backstage when illusionists were performing.

I once got a severe dressing down from the stage manager when I was up with the light operator on the "stage right" lighting platform; I got my head stuck in front of the light and it cast a shadow across the stage. Bobby Telford was on at the time but he was quite nice about it after.

My big debut, my one and only appearance in the Opera House, came in 1947. They knew that I played the accordion, and someone suggested that I should do a front curtain.

I was only fifteen and I played quite well on my own but I had never done a stage performance before and I was petrified. The walk from the wings to stage centre seemed like ten miles, and my hands felt like rubber gloves filled with water, I never saw the audience as my eyes went blurred.

I played a French Musette tune called *Nuits De Montmartre,* at least I think I did; it took about three minutes but it felt like three hours. I don't remember coming off.'

Cricket match at Venturefair with Opera House stars
Sidney Wilson, The Troy sisters et al with R.J. Walker, the manager

Brother and sister Margaret Tait and Ian Terris started going to The Opera House while she was too young to appreciate it, probably about the age of three, and spent at least part of the show asleep on her mother's lap.

When bored, Margaret would shuffle along the row to where the usherette sat on a little stool which folded back against the wall. Whenever she stood up it went back with a sharp *click*.

The family always sat in the circle and Ian remembered the blonde usherette standing under the green exit light, which shone on her blonde hair, making her look ethereal. When she was older, Margaret was stage-struck. She was a keen dancer and would like to have gone on the stage, but her mother disapproved.

'One of the Troy Sisters, Ivy, often came to our house for a meal, and I would go to the Opera House before the show with her to watch her put on her make-up.

In those days, mascara was in a block and you had to spit on it to dampen it, then use the end of a match stick to put it on your eyelashes.'

'The programme was always oriented round the comedian,' Ian said, 'everyone else was part of the supporting acts. During the war and early post war years it was Aly Wilson who was the star attraction and he was held in loving regard in the town.

He lived in digs with his wife and daughters in a flat above Tommy Black's shop in Douglas Street. His step-daughter, Berita, was a May Moxon Tiller-type girl. The Moxon Girls or Ladies almost all lived in the Buffie's Brae area.

Aly had a foil, Jimmy Lang, who always wore a grey double-breasted suit. The producer was Sid Wilson, a fine Scottish singer who didn't get the laud and honour that namesake Robert Wilson got, but was just as good. He sang as part of the act *The Troy Sisters and Wilson,* as well as a solo act.

The ice-breaker was always an accordion player, one was called Peter Cosimini. There was a xylophone act, two brothers. One was unfit for war service so carried on performing, and the other joined him when he was home on leave.

The Morelle Sisters

The one who wasn't called up played better but his clothes were shabby, while his brother was the opposite, his shirts spotless and his suits like new, but his playing showing lack of practice. Margaret preferred the comedy xylophone acts because a bunch of flowers always popped up out of the end of the instrument as the act finished, and was disappointed when this didn't happen.

On Saturday nights, The Opera House was a must. We always had seats booked and father's great ambition was to get centre advertising space on the safety curtain for his business, Stephen the Bakers, as it was Allan the Bakers who had it. When Allan's didn't renew their contract, father got in there quick. He felt he had arrived when he got that spot.

We had a car, a Wolseley 12, and even in those days you wouldn't leave the car out in the street while you went to the theatre. We drove it into Goodall's Garage in Queen Anne Street. There was no room to turn when you were in the garage so it went on to a turntable and was birled round to go back out again. Sometimes it was washed while we were at the show.

There were always queues in the street, and every man was wearing a 'bunnet'. Nearly everyone smoked at that time so the atmosphere must have been terrible but I have no memory of this. With reserved seats, we didn't have to queue and, as children, felt posh walking straight in.

My father must have been able to obtain additional seats for, whenever we had visitors, they were taken along as well. The audience knew precisely when the show was about to start. Arthur Lax, the musical director, was a very small man, and he would bob up and down three times, his head showing above the orchestra pit, to let the players know to commence playing on bob three.

Aly Wilson was my favourite, his motto was "Always Kidding". I remember seeing Dave Willis often enough with his little Hitler-type moustache. His son Denny Willis came in just as vaudeville was finishing.

The cast didn't just do their own thing, it was not enough to be a singer or a xylophone player, they all had little set pieces, comedies or tragedies, simple little things. We were easily amused in those days.

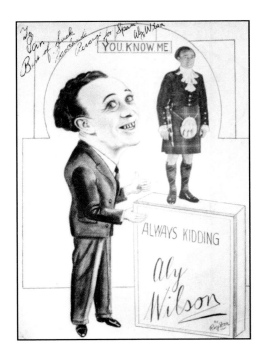

Aly Wilson

There was one I remember. A chorus girl, dressed up as an old lady in a shawl, is wondering how her son was getting on at the war.

A roll of drums and her son comes in with a bunch of flowers and sings *It's My Mother's Birthday Today.* Then comes the dreaded telegram scene - Missing in Action. But not to worry. Back comes the son with another bunch of flowers and sings another song, while the audience weeps floods of tears!

There was precious little serious drama in our era. I remember when I went to college in Glasgow, fellow students were very impressed when I told them I would be going to The Opera House on Saturday night. I rose immeasurably in their esteem. Little did they know that apart from its name, The Opera House bore little relation to serious entertainment.

Because we were friendly with cast members it was *de rigueur* for us to go backstage. We were given passes by Mr Walker, the manager, and we always thought it was wonderful and intimate to be able to go into the dressing rooms. We often had cast members at our house for tea and took them for a sail in our boat.

I remember once going to Blackness and when it was time to return, the engine wouldn't start. People started panicking that they wouldn't get back in time for the show, and Aly Wilson's hands were blistered and bleeding with his efforts to get it started.

Luckily they did make it and, as they say, the show went on.'

The O'Neill Sisters

Summer Show stars

CHAPTER NINE
THEY PLAYED DUNFERMLINE

Almost everyone who recalled the Opera House singled out the dancing girls for special mention.

From The Four Mystic Maids, The Embasssy Girls and The Sydney Steppers to The Bluebell Dancers, the Tiller Girls and of course The Moxon Girls, the dancers were the back bone of every show. They were usually also the hardest worked and worst paid of any performers.

Maidie Murray remembered arriving in Dunfermline on a Monday morning and buying a hot pie from the bakers across the way from The Opera House to keep her going through the day's rehearsals.

Greta Sutherland was a Moxon girl and her first engagement was an eight week summer season with Johnny Victory. There were eight girls in the troupe and they had to be versatile.

'We did high kicking, tap dance, ballet, even rifle drill like in the army and were very much a part of variety. We went all over the country, Perth, Dundee, Saltcoats, Belfast and were hard worked, more so than the top stars, off and on stage all the time. Performances were twice nightly with a matinee on Saturdays. We rehearsed twenty minutes on our own, then the same with the troupe. The act changed weekly and we rehearsed on Fridays for the next week's show.'

Monday was the worst day when costumes for the new show had to be sorted out and fitted, and many of the girls had to do their own alterations and queue up to use the iron. In bigger shows, there would be a wardrobe mistress and all washing, ironing and mending was taken care of. For the stage, girls used leg tan made from a mixture of red and yellow ochre, rosewater and glycerine.

They couldn't afford to buy tights so had bare legs even on the coldest days and dressing rooms, usually draughty and unheated, were sometimes home to the occasional rat. In many theatres, the dancers' dressing rooms were on the top floor so a lot of time was spent running up and down stairs. When they played village halls, very often the kitchen doubled as their dressing and rehearsal room.

Girls had a hard time. They lived out of suitcases, earned about two pounds a week and many were supporting children or parents. Chorus girls and dancers, like everyone else except perhaps the star billing act, had to pay their own fares and look for lodgings whenever they arrived in a new town. With lodgings costing between twenty five and thiry shillings a week, girls not only shared digs but beds as well, sometimes as many as four to a bed. Greta stayed with Ma Somerville in Douglas street.

Digs were important. Landladies have come in for a lot of stick, often deservedly the butt of jokes by many comedians but they were actually a very part of the entertainment business.

There were always more people needing rooms than landladies able to cope with them and who could provide a service which hotels and boarding houses wouldn't supply.

Theatricals kept odd hours, out all day rehearsing, all evening performing and returning home close to midnight for their one proper meal a day - if they were lucky. They also needed to wind down after the show so late nights were normal.

The Alexander Brothers

Some landladies provided a home from home, with warm beds and well cooked meals. Others had lists of regulations - no boyfriends, no smoking, no shoes to be worn indoors.

Some counted out the lumps of coal allowed and rooms were so cold that girls had to sleep in socks, scarves and earmuffs.

In spite of the hardships, however, the dancers like most entertainers remember only the good times, the comradeship and the laughter.

Dancers shared the bill with the top stars of the day and Greta's list included Harry Gordon, Alec Finlay, Robert Wilson, Lex Mclean, Billy Stutt, Clarke and Murray and Jimmy Logan.

'Harry Gordon was really a gentleman. Usually girls got thrown aside but not with him, or Robert Wilson, they were great. Everyone loved Robert Wilson, he would do twenty to thirty minute spots and the audience didn't want to let him go. It was great to play to a packed house.'

Greta liked the place so much she married a Dunfermline man and went to live there. Her last show was at the Edinburgh Palladium in 1956.

The Moxon Girls, run by May Moxon, the Madame Bluebell of Scottish theatre, were probably the most famous Scottish dance troupes.

Born in 1906, into a show business family in Glasgow, May became part of the family act, The Four McLeans, and first appeared on stage at the age of ten, but had to give up her stage career as a dancer after a serious car accident when she was twenty eight. Her leg was crushed so badly that doctors said it would have to be amputated.

May refused saying she would rather die than lose her leg and eventually learned to hobble around on crutches. She had to earn a living, dancing and the theatre were all she knew, so the first troupe of Moxon Girls was formed.

With two experienced dancers to help, she was able to train new dancers one by one, asking them to watch and do what the others did.

May provided the costumes and because there wasn't much money she made them herself on a treadle sewing machine which she pedalled with her good leg. From this small beginning, May developed a business which provided dancers for dozens of venues all over the country.

Galt's Agency agreed to give them a week's trial engagement at the Empress Theatre Glasgow and the troupe were so successful that they moved on to the Metropole Theatre in Stockwell where they stayed as resident dancers for a record one hundred weeks. It was the first such record in Scotland for a resident troupe.

A request from the Palladium Theatre for another eight girls meant she had to find new dancers and so it went on. Over the years, May trained many troupes of May Moxon Dancers, the May Moxon Young Ladies and May Moxon Lovelies some of whom were still dancing in the nineteen seventies.

May retired in 1975. Her girls were known as the Scottish Tiller Girls and at least one went on to join the Bluebell Girls in Las Vegas. At The Opera House, as in other places, local dance academies were used and the most promising dancers were invited to join May's troupe.

One of these was Margaret Logan. She began dancing at the age of seven, learning ballet, highland and tap won many medals and prizes, and was involved in performances in village halls throughout Fife.

'The Opera house was a big thing for us. When I was fourteen I got all the stars autographs. I wanted to go on the stage and when the pantomime was on, half a dozen girls were chosen to appear. I think Cinderella was the first I was in.

Some of the girls were chosen to join the Moxon Group, which was based in Glasgow. My uncle, who was a comedian and magician, said it was too hard a life for a young girl, and I was not allowed to go.

In the Opera House, there were two sets of dressing rooms on either side of the stage. Those who were there regular had their own places, but we were downstairs. It was like a long corridor with six of us sharing the same dressing room. For dancing displays we wore ordinary make up but, in the Opera House, it had to be grease paint. The girls showed us how it should be done and treated us like little sisters.

We got to sit at the side of the stage to watch the acts but one night, somebody must have touched something they shouldn't and all the lights went out. We were banned from watching after that.'

Another dancing famous troupe was The Dryburgh Girls, run by Grace Dryburgh, the wife of Lex Mclean. One regular patron of the theatre had fond memories of the girls.

'There was one called Betty Morwood, who came from Edinburgh. She used to appear naked on the stage at the Opera House in a scene called 'Famous Paintings'. All the lights were put out and then a spotlight would reveal a large gilt picture frame with Betty and her pals posing as the picture. There would be several of these and this was supposed to be art and, as I recall, it was very effective with the stage lighting.

Betty Morwood, in spite of this, was a very shy young girl. She lived in digs like her pals in a house in Albany Street.'

The Eight Dryburgh girls appeared with *Our New Winter Show* from November 1942 till April 1943 but, apparently, no newspaper review of the nude show exists.

Working conditions were difficult, with the chorus and dancers being very far down the pecking list.

They got the worst dressing rooms, had to wash, repair and alter their costumes, didn't get paid for rehearsals which were often held in cold, damp surroundings, and got no paid holidays. May Moxon, in old age, would recall when her girls were happy to be paid two to three pounds a week for dancing six nights a week for six weeks, with often a midnight matinee as well.

What she didn't say was that her girls had to sign a guarantee that they would not join Equity. Refusal would have meant losing their jobs.

When chorus girls did eventually join Equity, wages were doubled, but they were not in it for the money, but because, they said, it was a lovely business with mostly, lovely people.

One of the most famous local personalities to appear in the Opera House was Miss Nettie Dick, who produced and acted in a number of plays. She recalled with amusement the night she was sent to look for a missing member of the cast.

'The Dunfermline Amateur Dramatic Society was performing *The Man Who Stayed At Home*. Bill Paterson, known as Big Bill, was a goalkeeper with Dunfermline Athletic Football Club. It so happened that the last Saturday of our performance, he was very late in arriving.

As the youngest member of the cast, I was sent down to the stage door to watch for a taxi, getting mixed up with people rushing to get their seats because it was 'House Full'. The taxi arrived, the doors were flung open and out came this enormous man, still with his yellow goalie's jersey on, and covered with mud and bruises.

I rushed to get all the doors open, he rushed into the dressing room, got into his make-up and at curtain up, there he was in his place.

George Haldane, a drummer in the orchestra at the Opera House, was in fact the last drummer to play there.

One of his most abiding memories was of Hector Nicol, who like many others, made a fairly easy transition from Music Hall to the club scene, and went on to earn huge fees and a reputation as a scatological comedian.

'I knew Hector Nicol,' George recalled, ' he didn't get much money in the Opera House. He was doing his act one night, dancing about the stage and his teeth dropped out, hit the stage and bounced into the grand piano, which Arthur Lax, the bandmaster was playing.

Hector was standing with his hand over his mouth and we were all wondering what had happened.

His sister called from the wings 'Come off , you busy fool'. He had to wait till the end of the show before he got his teeth out of the baby grand.'

Nearly fifty years after her first appearance at the Opera House, Freda Drysdale's memory of it is almost perfect. Born at Crombie in 1924 Freda moved to the New Row in Dunfermline when she was three. From her earliest days she was surrounded by music. Her grandfather Fred Marshall was precentor in Queen Anne Street Church for seventeen years and was still singing on his eighty ninth birthday.

Freda began singing when she was four and by seven was a member of the Shepherd's Hall Choir. She graduated through Queen Anne School and Dunfermline Abbey choirs to become a member of the Music Institute and the Choral Union. The Music Institute at that time was a closed shop but telling them she was Fred Marshall's granddaughter opened lots of doors.

'I joined the sight reading class and later had my voice trained there by Miss A.V. McWhirter. I did six years in Grand Opera - Gluck's *Orpheus, The Beggars Opera, The Bartered Bride, Maritana,* and *Faust* with the starring role in *Carmen* in 1952.

That brought me lots of chances. I was cover girl that year for the Dunfermline Week Magazine, the official programme for Gala Week. Morris Allan asked me to pose for that photograph.

Archie McCullough and his wife Kathie Kaye invited me on to his Top of the Town Show, I did the *Seguidille* from Carmen, and that led to broadcast and television appearances.

Jimmy Logan was in the same show and I worked for him later at his Metropole Theatre in Glasgow, with Larry Marshall, Bill Tennant and Sally Logan. I also worked the cabaret scene with Jimmy's brother Buddy. He was a great entertainer.

I appeared with Jimmy Shand for nearly thirty years and with his son, as well as many other well known artistes, travelling the country doing cabaret. I played the Webster Hall in Arbroath and lots of other holiday places with The Alexander Brothers.

My husband Ken, was my accompanist and manager and we played in theatres and hotels all over the country, in The Tower Lounge and The Ocean Room in Blackpool, Old Time Music Hall, clubs around Newcastle and South Shields areas and the Borders. We used to do an act in one club, run down the road to the next, then back to the first one for the second half.

I loved going up north to Inverness and Aviemore because the audiences were so good, I was billed as the most popular entertainer in Inverness and learned to drink whisky at ceilidhs. I hated drink at that time but Ken said people would be offended if I refused. He told me just to lip it and give the rest to him. Well, I lipped it and liked it because it was the real pure malt!

At The Caberfeidh Restaurant in the Caledonian Hotel, I used to entertain European visitors who were doing the Land's End to John O'Groats tour. It was a real party every night. I would ask the different nationalities to shake hands with each other, then I'd sing a song of each country in their own language.

I'd do little interviews at some tables, which were usually quite entertaining. Before singing *Catari* one night, I asked if there were any Italians in the audience. One man put up his hand and after the song was over, I asked him where about in Italy he came from. He replied in broad Scots that he was the local chip shop man.

I used to work with the White Heather Club when they were on tour. Once in The Travel Club in Kirkcaldy I got a standing ovation, stepped back and fell over the drums.

When I got to my feet I went to the mike and announced that there would be a five shilling un-cover charge because they must have seen my black lace knickers! Before that I always just intro-duced my songs but after that I started doing one liners.

Once in Glasgow we had bookings at the Rang-ers Club, the Celtic Club and the Jewish Club all in one day so I went from *The Star o Rabbie Burns* through Danny Boy to *Havanagila*.

I tried to please everyone. In hotels, there were always coach tours and if Ken was playing we could be more spontaneous. It was more difficult if I had an orchestra but we tried to do special num-ber for birthdays, anniversaries and so on.

We did cabaret at Wee Jimmy's in Cowden-beath for over three years and the Provost's last Command Performance in the Carnegie Hall in Dunfermline.

We loved playing all the clubs around the Cow-denbeath, Lochgelly, Lochore, Kelty, Lumphin-nans and Cardenden area.

I was first taken to the Opera House when I was four and the second act I saw was Harry Lauder.

When I was thirteen I left school and went to work in Ogilvie's the hairdressers. It was the only shop in town that stocked greasepaint so all the ac-tors came in.

The shop got free passes for the Opera House so I went every week and sat in the front seats.   I got to know all the stars and Charlie Kemble once sang a ditty about me which began - *See that lassie sitting doon there.* I remember seeing Dave Willis as Hitler and him singing *Away, way up a kye.*

Freda by day...

Robert Wilson entertained the patients in the West Fife hospital in 1943 when he came to the Opera House. He came into the shop and asked if I liked his singing. I told him I like him better on Pathe Pictorial, but I was only fourteen. Everyone had great respect for Robert Wilson.

He later formed The White Heather Club which

...and Freda by night

he hosted with Andy Stewart. Ken and Alan Haynes were known as the most slick and well rehearsed duo ever to appear in Dunfermline. I remember them with Aly Wilson in Comedy Capers. Aly used to say *Keep the heid.*

I appeared twice at the Opera House with Jack Dougary, he had access to lots of wonderful local entertainers, especially from the Lochore area. *Freight Train* was his most popular number and we did shows all over the place from Princes Street gardens in Edinburgh to the Beach Pavilion in Leven.

I gave up in 1970 but remained semi-professional and all my memories are of music, although I did play the Second Witch in Macbeth with the Rex Deering Company in The Opera House in 1954. Rex Deering himself played Banquo and Denise Coffey was a page. Denise was stage struck even then. Later we would travel on the same eight o'clock train to Glasgow to start rehearsals in our different theatre.

Being with the Rex Deering Crown Players was a great thrill. Calum Mill was absolutely brilliant. He was in a television series at the time. Macbeth, or The Scottish Play is supposed to be unlucky. On the final night, the swordplay was so realistic that Calum got the tip of his thumb cut.

Years later, I went to see James Bell and he took me through the Opera House, by then turned into workshops. He had put a false ceiling on to the first level. It was sad to see the place go, I cried buckets when it was demolished.

A lot of people cut their acting teeth there. Companies used it as a stepping stone to bigger and better things. Some of the greatest acts in Music Hall appeared there at one time or another.

Freda was not the only person to remember the 1954 performance of Macbeth. Denise Coffey began her professional stage career at The Opera House before going on to became a household name as a radio, film and television performer. She starred alongside Phyllis Logan in *Another Time, Another Place* with Trevor Howard, in *Sir Henry at Rawlinson End* ; played Soberness Miller in *Far From The Madding Crowd*, and in *Waltz of the Toreadors*, played Peter Sellers daughter, with Prunella Scales as her sister.

Her list of television appearances is equally impressive - three years doing *Do Not Adjust Your Set*, which was a forerunner of the Monty Python Show; two series or *Girls About Town* with Peter Baldwin, later better known as Derek Wilton in *Coronation Street*, and three series of *End of Part One*, written by Andrew Marshall and David Renwick, who went on to write *One Foot in the Grave* for Thames TV.

She wrote, performed and co-produced a series of *Hold the Front Page,* made regular appearances in the Stanley Baxter Shows on BBC Scotland in the sixties and then on London ITV in the seventies. More television roles have been in *Casualty* and *Pie in the Sky*, while on radio she was an occasional guest on quiz shows such as *I'm Sorry I Haven't a Clue.*

Most of Denise's later work was in the USA and Canada and for more than eight years she directed many plays of Shaw and Noel Coward at Niagara-on-the-Lake, in Ontario; compiled a chamber opera based on Oscar Wilde's writings; she travelled through Canada and America, directing productions of Shakespeare and Shaw and lecturing to University students the length and breadth of the country, from Calgary to Wisconsin. In 1995, she was part of a project with veteran actors in Canada as Director *of A Midsummer Night's Dream.*

The following year Denise spent some time lecturing on Shakespeare at the University of Alberta directing The *Taming of The Shrew* at the prestigious Citadel Theatre in Edmonton, and then transferred the production to the National Arts Centre in Ottawa. By 2003, she was back in Britain, still working with BBC Radio.

Denise has fond memories of Fife in general and The Opera House in particular.

'My maternal grandparents ran the Royal Hotel in Inverkeithing from around 1912 to the late twenties, and my mother, with some of her family used to go to all the opening nights at the Opera House. The custom then, as now, was to invite local business people to be guests at the first performance because they would advertise the show by word of mouth.

After years of living in England and Scotland I went to Dunfermline High School in 1948. We moved to Milesmark in the early fifties by which time I was mad about theatre, so was able to go to whatever was playing at The Opera House and also to plays and concerts at the Carnegie Hall.

I think it was 1953 or early 1954, there was a production of Macbeth at The Opera House and a few of us from school were taken on as extras. The following year I was lucky enough to start my professional life in the theatre at The Opera House with The Rex Deering Crown Players.

They were a repertory company whose programme was a mixture of old-fashioned sentimental plays like *Peg O My Heart* and *The Rosary* and the latest gritty realist plays like *Age of Consent*.

I left Glasgow College of Drama in 1957 and was taken on as an interviewer and reporter on the innovative BBC radio programme *Scope* in Edinburgh. It was during my time there that the subject of the demolition of The Opera House came to our attention, so I seized the opportunity to interview myself on the programme.

I wrote to the Dunfermline Press to support many others who felt it should somehow be saved for a future part in the life of the town, and for its unique and beautiful painted auditorium. All praise to the people who worked so hard to succeed in delaying the demolition.

Many years later, by now working in USA and Canada, I met Iain Mackintosh, the architect of the new theatre in Calgary, Alberta, where I was directing a production.

I learned from him that although the shell of The Opera House had been long ago demolished, the interior and all its decoration had been preserved, being classed, I think, Grade II, and that it would soon be resurrected in Sarasota.

So it was that I went there, met the splendid woman, Elizabeth Lindsay and was there when the container was opened and the dusty old Fife cherubs blinked in the Florida sunshine, and the painted palm trees met the real thing.... there were tears in my eyes as I greeted them.

If I'd been able to choose what to put on for the opening performance, it would have been Jimmy Logan in his superb production about Harry Lauder. It was brilliant, appropriate and not too long. I know from other gala evenings that everything tends to run late. Unfortunately, I've never been back to see the finished splendour, but it's wonderful to know it's there and that the towns are linked.

Denise Coffey

Shortly after the demolition of the Opera House, Bill Gourlay and Gordon Ellis made a film about the theatre. Jimmy Logan, who was appearing at the Adam Smith Halls at the time, agreed to be interviewed and share his memories.

'The golden years of Scottish Music hall belonged to a time when people went out for their entertainment' he told them. 'Alec Finlay - I used to wash his car for sixpence. Tommy Morgan , Clairty Clairty , I'll never forget he used to say 'Is this no a posh hoose, they've even got fruit and naebody's sick.' Jack Anthony, he was my Uncle Jack. Tommy Lorne , 'I'll get ye and if I don't get ye, the coos will.' And a man who was a genius in his own time, Dave Willis.

In Scotland we love a good singer and few were more popular than Robert Wilson. He won many admirers with his singing in theatres from the Glasgow Empire to the London Palladium. And every show had its bevy of beautiful girls, The Tiller Girls and of course, The Moxon Girls.

There used to be a regular Charity Parade and I decided to ride a penny farthing bicycle through the streets and it was more difficult than I thought. I nearly killed myself because a penny farthing is very difficult to cycle.

If you push with your right foot, you're automatically pushing the wheel in the opposite direction to the one you want to go. You have to push and pull at the same time.

There was a portable fish and chip van with a horse and cart. How it didn't set fire to the whole wooden thing, I will never know. It was charcoal and the suppers were marvellous. I can taste them yet. I remember late one night the people I was with were desperate for a drink. I had a half bottle of whisky in my dressing room which I'd been saving. They said I had to get in.

Well, above the stage door was a window and I climbed up a rone pipe. The top half of the window opened down so got in but was hanging upside down over the toilet.

There's character in a theatre. You can try but it's very difficult to get it in a modern hall. The interior of the Opera House was a gem of course. It was the kind of theatre that if you stood on the stage and worked to the audience they were very close to you, and you could almost put your hands up and shake hands with people sitting in the boxes at the side.

I think for me, and for everyone else, buildings like these will never be replaced. That was the first theatre I wanted to buy. In all the things that are regarded as the standards of life we should try and attain, a theatre with all its shades of drama, comedy and pantomime, makes a town a better place to live in.

Some people, like Aberdeen, realised what a precious building they had, which can never be repeated. Edinburgh and Glasgow have taken the theatres built around 1907 and restored their complete beauty and made use of them to contribute to the life of the community.

You will never replace the Opera House, and the community will not regret it as much as they should, but years from now, they'll regret it bitterly.'

When Brian Nobile was arranging the exhibition in 2000, he wrote to a number of stars who had appeared in Dunfermline, and Jimmy was among them. He was still enthusiastic about the coal fired chip van and his appearances in Dunfermline, and had apparently forgiven those responsible for demolishing the theatre.

'My memories of the Opera House, Dunfermline go back to 1945 when I played in the Summer Season there with George Burton as the comedian, and a nice lady, Billy Brown, on accordion. I was about sixteen and in digs sharing with George Burton.

We all wore the Perriot Costumes in the opening as a tradition established about 1936 when they had a great success. I think they hoped it would bring them luck each year.

The stage was a good size and backstage there was a small side room near the front entrance of the stage with seating around that those who were waiting to go on could sit and wait in comfort.

Being an old music hall there was a wooden stair up to a door which opened in half and had a small shelf as a counter and looked into the upstairs Public Bar. I presumed this allowed some of the acts when they were appearing in Variety to have a drink when they felt like it.

I bought a motor cycle and it was so old and needed so much work on it that I only managed to ride to Glasgow and I don't think it ever made any other journey as the fork was cracked.

I remember standing outside the theatre a couple of years later in the evening with a friend trying to persuade him to buy it as it was for sale. I think I spoke of seven thousand pounds. I was about seventeen or eighteen at the time and didn't have even thousand pennies, but the thought was beautiful.

I travelled to Sarasota in Florida a few years ago and saw the restored interior of the Opera House and it is beautiful.

They are full of pride at the lovely theatre in America. When I told them I was coming and had appeared in the theatre, they thought I would have a wheel chair or a zimmer.'

Robert The Bruce in his new home

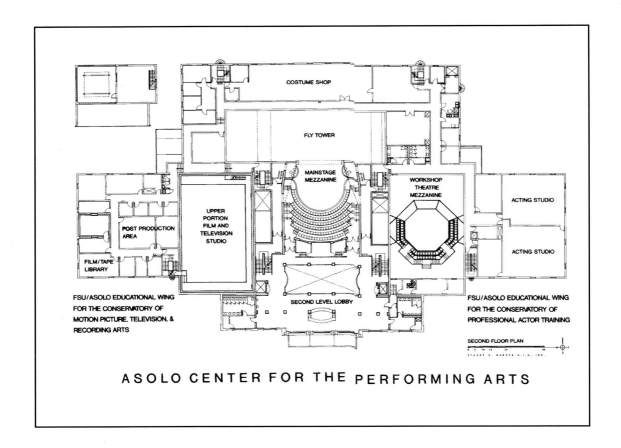

ASOLO CENTER FOR THE PERFORMING ARTS

Plans of The Asolo Center

CHAPTER TEN

SISTER CITIES AND CENTENARIES

'What a unique way to celebrate our founding fathers and our roots by adopting a Scottish city.

Dunfermline is a perfect partner and 'sister', highlighted by our special connection through its former opera house that now serves as the core of our Florida State performing Arts Centre and home of the Asolo Theatre Company.'

Linda Rosenbluth
President, Sarasota Sister Cities Association

Dunfermline is no stranger to the idea of partnership with other cities. It first 'twinning', with Trondheim took place in 1947 and the links of friendship and co-operation remain strong.

The Sister Cities concept was developed in America in 1956, by President Eisenhower. Its purpose was to increase international co-operation and understanding by promoting communication at the person to person level, through city to city affiliations.

Sarasota wished to develop links with other people and cities with a similar and cultural environment, so the Sarasota Sister Cities Association was formed in 1963 through a relationship with San Domingo in the Dominican Republic.

Other links followed, with Hamilton in Canada, Perpignon in France, Tel Mond in Israel, and Vladimir in Russia. In 2001, Dunfermline was added to the list

On Monday October 14, 2002, the City of Sarasota and the Sarasota Sister Cities association held a reception and dinner to celebrate the hundredth anniversary of their city, and the formal signing of the 'twinning' agreement with Dunfermline.

This was the culmination of a process begun just over a year earlier, when the Sister City relationship was formed and a commitment made to friendship, and to the development of municipal, organisational and personal relations in culture, education, trade, professional fields and other areas of interest.

Tom Dair, Convenor of Fife Council, had no doubt that the bond already formed between the two cities with Sarasota's acquisition of the Dunfermline Opera House was one of the driving forces towards the agreement. He explained how the twinning came about.

'Twinning was almost a spontaneous initiative generated by people who had been to Sarasota, who had visited the old Opera House in its new situation, and made new friends there.

A meeting was held in the offices of the Carnegie Trust so the twinning group was genuinely created from the community of Dunfermline. It was a well attended meeting, officers were appointed, and those persons pledged themselves to both the principle and objective of founding a twinning link with Sarasota.

That decision was then transmitted to the people of Sarasota, who were already looking for twinning links in Scotland.

The original area the Sarasotans looked at was Aberdeenshire, because they had some kind of relationship with the Clan Gordon. However, after an exploratory visit to Fife, the recommendation came down firmly on establishing a sister city link between Dunfermline and Sarasota.

In August 2001, when Sarasota City Commissioners and representatives of their Sister Cities Association visited Dunfermline, I was pleased to be a signatory on behalf of the city and the citizens of Fife at the first signing ceremony in the City Chambers.

The second half of the ceremony took place in the Van Wezel Performing Arts Hall in Sarasota, in an auditorium which I believe holds about eight or nine thousand people.

Everything was correctly and efficiently done by the City Commissioners and once again, I was a signatory along with the Mayor of Sarasota.

The signing ceremony left to right : Don Osborne, Gerry McMullen, Tom Dair, Mayor Carolyn Mason, Linda Rosenbluth, Bill Wallace

Those signing on behalf of the Sister Cities Association were Linda Rosenbluth for Sarasota and Gerry McMullan for Dunfermline.'

Tom Dair was enthusiastic about the benefits to both cities from the twinning arrangement.

'There are much more than social advantages to be gained,' he said, 'People in Sarasota are looking to form economic links with Dunfermline.

The City Commission and the person appointed as its representative, have already been in discussion with people here about the industrial background of Fife, what's here and what might be explored.

We plan to have educational exchanges. Sarasota has one of the finest educational set ups anywhere in the United States, and there will be opportunities for young people, schoolchildren and students, to exchange and share each others cultures.

The School of Art and Design in Sarasota is world class, people from all over the world attend courses there and we now have direct links with it through our new Sister City relationship.

Plans are still in the early stages but the biggest economic advantage is the spending power of tourism. At the moment, most of the tourist traffic is going one way, to the States, but we are promoting Dunfermline, Fife and Scotland through this link with the Sister Cities association.

Obviously the tourism aspect is important, but it is much wider than that. Dunfermline is now on the tourist map and a number of Sarasotans will be coming here to research their Scottish ancestry.

The Heritage Trust should be able to take advantage of that and we are looking to show our visitors the best.

Sarasota is only one hundred years old, so for people to walk into the City Chambers in Dunfermline and see plaques of provosts going back to the fifteenth century is to give some idea of the age of the place.'

One of the high points of Tom Dair's visit to America was going to see the old Opera House in its new surroundings.

'I used to visit the Opera House regularly, and remember the acts, Chic Murray and Maidie especially. I always had a desire, which was never fulfilled to sit in one of those grand boxes at the side of the stage. When I went to Sarasota, they opened up one of the boxes, let me in and fulfilled a lifetime ambition.

I gave them a new word to use. We did a ceremony in the Opera House along with the Commissioners and the Sister Cities Group. On the stage, you could see the different levels, the balcony and what they called the upper balcony.

I advised them that in Dunfermline it was referred to as 'the Gods', because you were nearer to God than the stage, and that brought a bit of hilarity into the proceedings.

Having been in the Opera House in Dunfermline, walking into that beautiful building made you feel as if you had moved into a time warp. They have certainly done us proud.

Whoever was responsible for insisting that the bulldozers should not be put through the building till these parts were saved, did us a huge favour.

It is absolutely gorgeous, the emotional feeling of nostalgia just sweeps over you, seeing something you thought had gone forever restored in that fashion.

As you go in, there is a brass rubbing of Robert the Bruce taken from his grave in Dunfermline Abbey.

These brass rubbings are taken all across the country but this is the only one in the United Kingdom where the person represented is wearing a crown. It is full length, standing on display just as you go into the building.

It is not only an attractive asset in that theatre building, it is also an encouragement for people to come and see the city and burgh of Dunfermline as it was.'

Sarasota may be only one hundred years old, without the history and old world charm of Dunfermline but they do know how to put on a good show.

Bill Wallace, who along with Don Osborne, is a Director of Dunfermline City, described the centenary and twinning event as a huge success.

Writing in the Sarasota Sister Cities newsletter, he said it was the first time that representatives of all the sister cities had gathered together.

'Ceremonial highlight of their six day visit was the Monday evening dinner, and the signing of documents on the stage of the Van Wesel Performing Arts Hall, which officially proclaimed that Dunfermline had become Sarasota's newest sister city.

The ceremony was replete with pipers and a handsome display of tartans from the Caledonian Clubs collection. Sarasota Mayor Carolyn Mason and Fife Council's Convenor, Tom Dair, Sister City President Linda Rosenbluth and Dunfermline's Twinning Chairman Gerald McMullan inked the formal documents.

The performance that evening of *'Celebrate Sarasota'* was acclaimed as 'one of the finest entertainments ever offered in the long history of the Van Wesel Performing Hall.'

Wallace went on to explain that the focus of the event, as well as ushering in the city's second century, was to develop future exchanges of programmes and people in the areas, among others of business, the arts, education, athletics, religion, film making, horticulture and history.

Undoubtedly the Sister City ceremony was a historic occasion, but it should be remembered that history is not just about world shattering events. It is also about the little, seemingly unimportant things, without which the big events would not be possible.

Sarasota celebrated its centenary in October 2002. It is barely a year older than the interior of its theatre, which saw its opening performance on September 11,1903.

The history of the Dunfermline Opera House could have ended in 1955, when the curtain came down on the last show.

Instead, thanks to the foresight of the few – people like Bill Gourlay and Gordon Ellis who recorded its last days; Iain Mackintosh and Sir James Dunbar-Nasmith who fought to preserve, first the building then, when that was deemed impossible, to save the unique plaster work; and to the people of the Asolo who recognised its quality – it, too, is about to embark on its second century.

BIBLIOGRAPHY

Music Hall Memories - Jack House   Richard Drew Publishing Glasgow 1986

The Waggle of The Kilt - Karen Marshalsay   Glasgow University Library - 1992

Aberdeen Tivoli - J.H. Littlejohn   Rainbow Books - Aberdeen - 1986

Scottish Showbusiness - Frank Bruce NMS publishing Ltd - Edinburgh 2000

Kindly Leave The Stage, The Story of Variety 1919 1960 - Roger Wilmutt   Methuen London - 1985

The Good Auld Days - Gordon Irving Jupiter Books, London, 1977

Roy Hudd's Cavalcade of Variety Acts - Roy Hudd & Philip Hindin   Robson Books - London 1977

Curtains !!!or A New Life For Old Theatres – Iain Mackintosh and Michael Sell (editors) John Offord (Publications) Ltd 1988

Kings Queens and Picture Palaces - Vivien Devlin   Polygon 1991

British Music Hall, An Illustrated Who's Who from 1850 to the Present Day – Roy Busby

The Ayr Gaiety – Johnny Moore Albion Press 1976

ABOUT THE AUTHOR

Lillian King is a graduate of Edinburgh University with an MA in English and History, is an editor and publisher and a part time WEA tutor of history and creative writing. Books include

A Railway Childhood; The Last Station; Famous Women of Fife ;
Sair, Sair Wark, Women and Mining in Scotland;
Thornton Railway Days

Brian Nobile is an entertainment historian with a special interest in Fife's musical and theatrical history , has researched variety, folk and popular artistes who have appeared in Dunfermline and contributed to the entertainment and boxing sections of *Twentieth Century Dunfermline.*

PICTURE ACKNOWLEDGEMENTS

Photographs and illustrations are reproduced by kind permission of the following

Carnegie Library, Dunfermline	3, 13
Brenda Kucharewski	23, 28, 44, 50, 58, 62, 101,106, 108,109
Mr & Mrs James Matson	85, 86,
Ian Terris	98, 108
Margaret Tait	76 lower, 77 lower
Archie Foley	16, 34, 42, 48
Linda Rosenbluth	121, 124
Brian Nobile	18, 20, 27, 32, 47, 53, 80, 108,
Mrs Jimmy Logan	57
J. H. Littlejohn	25, 36,54,
Bill Gourlay & Gordon Ellis	64, 67, 69, 70, 73,74 l, 75 l, 76 u, 77u, 78u, 79u , 94
Freda Drysdale	107, 116,117
The Alexander Brothers	112
Denise Coffey	119
Iain Mackintosh	122
The Dunfermline Press Group	15,61
The Dunfermline Journal	8
Wayne Eastep	74 right, 75 right, 78 lower, 79 lower
Dunfermline City Chambers	38
Johnny Beattie	4
Arlene McMechan	46
Andy Hamilton	96